THE LENOX SCHOOL OF JAZZ

A Vital Chapter in the
History of American Music and Race Relations

Also by Jeremy Yudkin

UNDERSTANDING MUSIC

MILES DAVIS, "MILES SMILES,"
AND THE INVENTION OF POST BOP

MUSIC IN MEDIEVAL EUROPE

DISCOVER MUSIC

THE LENOX SCHOOL OF JAZZ

A Vital Chapter in the History of American Music and Race Relations

Jeremy Yudkin

Published for
THE LENOX LIBRARY ASSOCIATION
by Farshaw Publishing
on the occasion of the Lenox Library's 150th Anniversary

Printed in the United States of America
Design by Eileen Rosenthal Graphic Design

ISBN 0-9789089-1-0

Farshaw Publishing
A division of Keep-A-Head, Inc.
43 Main Street
Post Office Box 415
South Egremont MA 01258

Library of Congress Control Number: 2006934344

ACKNOWLEDGMENTS

I am extremely grateful to the Lenox Library and its entire staff, especially its Executive Director, Denis Lesieur; Executive Assistant and Volunteer Coordinator, Lisa Berkel; and its development officers Ginger Schwartz and Jennifer Kinney. They have been so welcoming, helpful, and supportive during the process of my writing this book. The research librarians Amy Lafave and Adrienne Wesson were not only extraordinarily responsive to my requests but active in guiding any relevant items my way. The Lenox Library is a wonderful place – a jewel among libraries. It celebrates its 150th birthday this year, and I am honored to be the author whose work has been chosen as part of the commemoration of this signal event.

Arthur Collins, the husband of the late Stephanie Barber, made himself available for countless hours of conversation and questioning and allowed me access to the rich and valuable archive he and Stephanie's sons have donated to the Library. I appreciate very much his openness, warmth, and quick intelligence.

George Schuller was generous enough to read through my entire manuscript and make detailed suggestions based on his own research for the documentary film on Music Inn. I am very grateful to him.

My thanks are due also to Michael Selzer of Farshaw Publishing and to designer Eileen Rosenthal, who is responsible for the fine appearance of this book. Both were a pleasure to work with.

Finally, I am delighted to take this opportunity to thank my supportive family, especially my wonderful wife Kathryn and my heart-warming children, Daniel and Susanna.

TABLE OF CONTENTS

INTRODUCTION

The most vibrant period in the entire history of American jazz was that between 1949 and 1960. More musical styles arose and competed for attention in the 1950s than in any other: Swing, Bop, Cool, West Coast, Hard Bop, Mainstream, Third Stream, Modal, and Free all had their exponents and their adherents. Rising stars included Miles Davis, John Coltrane, Dave Brubeck, and Ornette Coleman. Enjoying renewed attention were established soloists and bandleaders such as Louis Armstrong, Duke Ellington, and Count Basie, while real old-timers like ragtime pianist Eubie Blake were still playing up a storm. The revival of New Orleans-style music, under the name of Traditional jazz, was attracting audiences and filling clubs. Much of the history of American jazz in that period took place on one of the two coasts: New York was the undisputed capital of jazz performance, recording, and publishing, while Los Angeles and San Francisco were venues for new clubs and some important jazz labels. But there were also important centers of jazz in Chicago, Philadelphia, and Detroit.

The rise of jazz in the Fifties coincided with important changes in the social and cultural fabric of the United States. The immediate postwar years of rebound and recovery had given way to a period of considerable prosperity. And America was feeling its way out of a centuries-long dependence on Europe and towards cultural and artistic self-reliance. A largely conformist society provided an opportunity for rebellion and independence. Counter-culture icons were movie actor James Dean and *Catcher in the Rye*'s Holden Caulfield; while in real life members of the "Beat" generation, Jack

Kerouac, William Burroughs, and Allen Ginsberg stood for personal freedom, intensity, and commitment. For much of the decade music represented youth's most energetic locus of independence. Whether swing dancing to the big bands or frequenting small bop clubs, young people found liberation in music and idols of cool in jazz soloists such as Miles Davis. During those few years the fount of culture making changed hands from the middle class to the working class, from the middle aged and settled to the young and restless, and from white to black.

This book tells the story of the Lenox School of Jazz, a historic institution in rural Massachusetts, which ran only from 1957 to 1960 and only in the summers but had a profound effect on the history of American jazz and the formation of the American soul. This was the place where composer and pianist John Lewis worked as music director for several seasons; where jazz scholar and composer Gunther Schuller wrote and taught; where saxophonist and clarinetist Jimmy Giuffre played and recorded; where Dizzy Gillespie played his trumpet up in a tree ("I've always wanted to play in a tree," said Gillespie),[1] and where the modern jazz saxophonist Ornette Coleman came to (spectacular) public attention. It was also the place where black teachers taught white students, where white audiences came to hear black performers in a dignified setting, and where white and black musicians mingled in a situation of unqualified collegiality.

The story is one of vision and energy, of enthusiasts, scholars, performers, and teachers coming together in common purpose. It is the story of racial harmony in an era of taut racial tension. A story of legendary music making, some of which is captured in historical recordings. And it is the story of a soft-spoken, determined, flamboyant, intelligent, forward-thinking woman, who made most of it happen.

Chapter 1

Social and Cultural Background of the Fifties

The Lenox School of Jazz was an outgrowth of seminars and roundtable discussions held at the Music Inn in Lenox, a small but notable town in the Berkshire hills of western Massachusetts. The Inn was established in 1950 by Stephanie and Philip Barber, who had come from New York City to the Berkshires to find a weekend retreat and ended up creating a prestigious and influential home for jazz and other American popular music. In the beginning the Barbers hosted a small discussion group of folk and jazz performers and scholars at the Inn; but by the late Fifties Music Inn was hosting a summer-long series of folk and jazz concerts, featuring some of the most important jazz stars of the day, including Louis Armstrong, Duke Ellington, Count Basie, Dave Brubeck, Stan Kenton, George Shearing, Sarah Vaughan, the Modern Jazz Quartet, and Sonny Rollins.

The School of Jazz was the brainchild of the Barbers and of John Lewis, the jazz composer and pianist who led the Modern Jazz Quartet for over forty years. Although it was only a short summer program, and although it only lasted for four years, the Lenox School of Jazz attracted some of the most important performers, teachers, and scholars of the day. Performers who taught at Lenox included all four members of the Modern Jazz Quartet – John Lewis, vibraphonist Milt Jackson, bassist Percy Heath, and drummer Connie Kay – who were in residence at the School; pianist and composer Dave Brubeck, who used to live with his family at Music Inn during the summer; clarinetist/composer/ saxophonist Jimmy Giuffre, who ended up buying a house and living in the Berkshires; trumpeters Dizzy Gillespie, Freddie Hubbard, Kenny Dorham, and Booker Little; pianists Oscar Peterson and Bill Evans; guitarists Jim Hall and Herb Ellis; bassists Ray Brown, Chuck Israels, Ralph Peña, and Art Davis; trombonist/composer/pianist Bob Brookmeyer; trombonist J. J. Johnson; saxophonists Lee Konitz, George Coleman, Don Heckman, and Ed Summerlin; tuba player Ray Draper; and drummer Max Roach. Teaching composition at the School were composer and theorist George Russell and composer and arranger Bill Russo. Herb Pomeroy, the trumpeter and arranger and educator, taught ensemble. And two scholars who worked at the School were jazz historian and English professor Marshall Stearns, who lectured on jazz history; and Gunther Schuller, composer, arranger, and scholar, who lectured on jazz analysis and the relationship between jazz and classical music.

During its four-year span the School taught over one hundred and fifty students, of whom a number went on to distinguished careers in jazz. Most prominent among them are jazz educator David Baker, who is professor of jazz studies at Indiana University and the author of many jazz theory textbooks; pianist and composer

Ran Blake, who teaches at the New England Conservatory of Music; Jamey Aebersold, who runs a large business of jazz publications and instructional recordings; singer, pianist, and composer Bob Dorough; trumpeter, band-leader, and composer Don Ellis (d. 1978), who wrote the score for the movie *The French Connection*; pianist, teacher, and lyricist Margo Guryan; music journalist Don Heckman; pianist Steve Kuhn, who played briefly with John Coltrane; Arif Mardin, a long-time producer and arranger at Atlantic Records; bassist Larry Ridley, who was a professor at Rutgers University; composer, pianist, and author Tupper Saussy, who wrote *The Miracle on Main Street*; and drummer and composer ("How My Heart Sings") Earl Zindars.

Perhaps the most famous alumni of the Lenox School of Jazz are Don Cherry and Ornette Coleman, who together turned the jazz world upside down when their quartet (with Charlie Haden, bass, and Billy Higgins, drums) appeared at the Five Spot Café in New York, playing a kind of jazz that nobody had ever heard before, free of the conventional harmonic trajectory. Trumpeter Cherry, who died in 1995, was a pioneer in incorporating world music into jazz and led a series of groups based mostly in Europe. Ornette Coleman is one of the most famous figures in modern jazz. His innovations and originality have been among the most influential elements in jazz over the last fifty years. He was awarded the first Guggenheim Fellowship for jazz composition, won a $360,000 Mac Arthur Foundation "genius" award, and was inducted into *Down Beat*'s Hall of Fame. In 2005 the jazz world celebrated Coleman's 75th birthday with a series of concerts across Europe and the United States. With a new group, including his son Denardo on drums, Ornette Coleman is playing more intensely and beautifully than ever. But it was at the Lenox School of Jazz in 1959 that Coleman first came to spectacular public attention.

Lenox is an important town for other cultural reasons than jazz, however, for straddling the borders of both Lenox and Stockbridge lies Tanglewood, the summer home of the Boston Symphony Orchestra and the site one of the most important summer-long classical music festivals in the world. Our story involves the relationship, both admiring and strained, between the two musical institutions.

The Barbers would surely not have been attracted to Lenox had it not been for the classical music and other cultural attractions of the area. And the School's Board of Trustees included the brilliant conductor Leonard Bernstein, whose principal gig was down the road at Tanglewood, but who was known to spend evenings hanging out at the Music Inn. On the other hand, events at Music Inn had to be carefully timed not to clash with those at Tanglewood, and patronage dollars were jealously guarded by the Boston Symphony Orchestra.

Our story, like all stories in the history of jazz, also touches on race, for year-round inhabitants of Lenox as well as summer visitors were (and still are) unused to the sight of African-Americans wandering the streets and visiting the shops of the area. Local inns, hotels, and restaurants were highly unlikely to accept black guests; indeed most of them were still "restricted," turning away Jews and others not fitting into the mold of Fifties convention.

Indeed part of the intrigue of this story involves the historical, cultural, and societal context in which the Lenox School of Jazz operated, for the Fifties in America were the site of a continual contest between conformity and alienation. Television shows such as "Leave It to Beaver," "I Love Lucy," and "Father Knows Best" purveyed an image of America that was suburban, white, and highly conformist. But the image was narrowly focused, like the thin beam of a dated home movie, leaving much of the rest of the room in darkness. The image was completely missing one vital element: black people. Millions of black Americans lived in abject poverty in rural shantytowns or all-black districts in urban centers. Suburban developments simply did not sell houses to African Americans. Throughout the South there were separate facilities for blacks and whites, including drinking fountains. Black people had to use separate entrances to hotels and restaurants, if they were served at all. Schools were rigorously segregated. All this despite the ruling in the Fourteenth Amendment to the Constitution that state governments could not deny black citizens due process or equal protection and despite the 1954 Supreme Court ruling that "in the field of public opinion the doctrine of 'separate but equal' has no place." Black people were still brutalized or murdered in the South. The vicious, cold-blooded murder of Emmett Till, a fourteen-year-old boy, in 1955, was only the most notorious of thousands of incidents of violence and brutality. In Little Rock, Arkansas, in 1957, a high school was integrated by federal troops and at the point of a gun. In 1958 two black males were present when one of them was kissed by a white girl. They were arrested, convicted of attempted rape, and sentenced to 12 and 14 years in prison. The convicts were boys aged 7 and 9.

Black preachers (Martin Luther King), athletes (Willie Mays and Hank Aaron in baseball; Bill Russell and Wilt Chamberlain in basketball; fullback Jim Brown in football, and Althea Gibson in tennis) and the occasional black actor (Sydney Poitier) were slowly (painfully slowly!) changing American attitudes. But the principal locus of white admiration for black Americans has always been in jazz. So the jazz musician presented a double image to whites: the image of strangeness, exoticism, and fear, and at the same time the image of a truthteller, a carrier of emotional secrets, a prophet. The tensions of the Fifties, between black and white, between conformity and rebellion, were reflected in jazz.

Dave Brubeck and Eugene Wright (bass) performing at the Lenox School of Jazz in the late Fifties.

Jazz is truly a special language. Jazz says "what's on everybody's mind . . . filling empty space with the substance of our lives," as Jack Kerouac wrote in *On the Road*. And the Lenox School of Jazz was the place where this language could be learned, where white students learned from black teachers, black and white musicians learned from each other, and a feeling of mutual respect enveloped students and teachers alike. "There was a real atmosphere of scholarship and dignity," says Sonny Rollins of the School. "There's no place quite like it now." [1]

Lenox and the Black Musician

The School of Jazz established itself in the unusual small-town atmosphere of Lenox, Massachusetts. Lenox is the center of what is now a thriving cultural area in the Berkshire Hills on the border between Massachusetts and New York State. It is equidistant from New York and Boston (about three hours by car), a town of about six thousand inhabitants, whose population swells significantly in the summers as a result of the beauty of the countryside and the cultural offerings of the area. Billed as "America's Premier Cultural Resort," the Berkshires offers nationally renowned museums, such as the Norman Rockwell Museum and the Sterling and Francine Clark Art Institute; theater companies, such as Shakespeare and Company, the Barrington Stage Company, the Berkshire Theater Festival, and the Williamstown Theatre Festival; dance at Jacob's Pillow; and music all over the place but principally at Tanglewood, the summer home of the Boston Symphony Orchestra. Many of these institutions have histories that go back to the 1920s and 1930s. Tanglewood itself began operation in 1935.

The beautiful Berkshires.

The Berkshires was a recreational area long before that, however. In the mid-nineteenth century, authors and poets found tranquillity for their work in western Massachusetts. Herman Melville wrote *Moby Dick* in his Berkshire home, and Nathaniel Hawthorne spent a year in the Berkshires, working on his *Tanglewood Tales* and *The House of the Seven Gables*. In the last decades of the century many of the bankers and tycoons who had become rich from the industrial age built spectacular "cottages" in the Berkshires, which rivaled their city homes in size, grandeur, and luxury. Industrialist

Ventfort Hall in Lenox, built in 1893, with twenty-eight rooms.

Giraud Foster, for example, built a house in Lenox that was a copy of the *Petit Trianon* palace of King Louis XV of France![1] Thus the Vanderbilts, Carnegies, Tappans, Winthrops, Choates, and other rich families established an atmosphere of elegant living and high culture amidst the meadows, pine forests, and lakes of the Berkshire Hills.

In 1887 Clark W. Bryan wrote a book about the Berkshires with the following delightful title: *The Book of Berkshire, Describing and Illustrating its Hills and Homes, and Telling Where They Are, What They Are and Why They Are Destined to Become the Most Charming and Desirable Summer Homes in America. For the Season of 1887.*[2] In it, he waxes lyrical about the place: "Its beauties of form, its favorable features of landscape, and its pictures of loveliness, in combination, are unsurpassed. . . ."[3] "Another region may be found

18

conspicuous for imposing wildness, another that is pretty, possibly beautiful; others may be healthful and invigorating, pleasant places for summer sojourn and interesting in their surroundings, where guests may find agreeable provision for their comfort and enjoyment; but there is not another region with which Berkshire must divide the honor of having all these at once. . . ."[4] In 1933 Mabel Dodge Luhan wrote about the Lenox she had known as a child in the 1890s:

> Lenox was a small tender village at the bottom of a bowl. Great hills rolled all about it, that grew brilliant with color in the fall. The hills were dotted here and there with enormous "places" [mansions], silent and serious among the trees, but the village was quietly alive and had a lively sweetness about it.[5]

The story of the School of Jazz mirrors the story of America's recovery and resurgence during the postwar years, for the growing economy allowed more time for leisure and cultural pursuits, while young people saw in jazz an escape from conformity. Jazz wove its riffs through the rhythms of the Beat poets and the novels of Angry Young Men like Jack Kerouac. Kerouac's novel *On the Road* (1957) tells the story of a wild, restless ride across the country, searching for alcohol, drugs, and love, but mostly for meaning. It contains delighted descriptions of jazz and is improvisatory in feel. Even more so is his writing in a 1955 piece entitled "Jazz of the Beat Generation," in which his paragraph-long sentences rise and fall in rhythmic delight like a great jazz solo. In this piece he hymns Lester Young, Count Basie, Louis Armstrong, and Miles Davis in a single sentence, describing Young as "the greatness of America in a single Negro musician . . . blow[ing] all Kansas City to ecstasy."[6] Ginsberg first made his name with the publication of his long poem

Howl (1956), which mourns the destruction of "the best minds of my generation" by materialism and conformity, nods to Kerouac in its opening line, and goes on a wild improvisatory rampage like a great honking tenor.[7]

For many leaders and followers of the counter culture, it was only in blackness that the requisite elements of authenticity, genuine feeling, and otherness could be located.[8] Norman Mailer equated the virtues of blackness with hipness in his 1957 essay "The White Negro."[9] The New York poet Frank O'Hara wrote that he wanted to think of himself as black: "I consider myself to be black . . . ."[10] Kerouac elaborated in *On the Road*: "At lilac evening I walked with every muscle aching among the lights of 27th and Welton in the Denver colored section, wishing I were a Negro, feeling that the best the white world had offered was not enough ecstasy for me, not enough life, joy, kicks, darkness, music, not enough night."[11] Jerry Leiber and Mike Stoller, the great song-writing team of the Fifties, were responsible for many of the hits of the time, including "Real Ugly Woman," "Hound Dog," "Searchin'," "Yakety Yak," "Dance with Me," and "Love Potion No. 9." Leiber remembered that LeRoi Jones (Amiri Baraka) once referred to them as "the only authentic black voices in pop music." He said that they were flattered: "I think we wanted to be black."[12] For white hipsters and suburban youngsters alike, the canonical figure of expression and intensity was the black musician.

The Barbers and the Music Inn

It is important for the reader to keep clear the distinction between the Lenox School of Jazz and the Music Inn in Lenox. The School of Jazz was one of the programs of The Music Inn, which was a resort that Philip and Stephanie Barber opened in 1950. The New York couple bought a group of outbuildings on the property of a magnificent mansion, known as Wheatleigh, built in 1897 at the height of the Gilded Age. The mansion was built as a wedding present to his daughter by her father, Chicago banker and railway magnate, Henry Cook, when she married the Count de Heredia of Paris. The countess lived there for nearly fifty years. The mansion is spectacular, modeled as it is on a sixteenth-century Italian palazzo, with thirty-three rooms, interior walls built with two layers of brick, twelve intricately carved stone fireplaces, marble bathrooms, a majestic winding staircase, and Tiffany windows. Outdoors, the grounds, designed by Frederick Law Olmstead (the designer of New York's Central Park), are ornamented by gardens, balustrades, porticoes, and terraces. The wedding was elaborate and was described by the *New York Times* as "one of the prettiest celebrated this season." The bride's dress was of white brocaded silk. "It was cut with Court train, high neck, and long sleeves. The front was of white satin, covered with chiffon, festooned with orange blossoms and point lace."[1] The mansion was added to the National Register of Historic Places in 1982. From 1921 to 1943 (when gasoline restrictions put a stop to them), the Countess hosted outdoor Sunday evening sunset services on the grounds of Wheatleigh sponsored by the Trinity Episcopal Church of Lenox.

The Countess died in 1946, some thirty years after her husband, and the estate was divided. In 1947 the Boston Symphony Orchestra bought the main house and twenty-five acres to use as a dormitory for its Tanglewood students. The outbuildings of the property and one hundred acres of land were purchased by the Barbers in 1950. Philip Barber was one of the owners of a public relations firm in New York – Barber and Barr – but he was artisti-

Wheatleigh mansion, built in 1897.

cally inclined, having written plays, taught drama at Yale, and authored one of the standard books on scene designing.[2] He had also worked as the director of the Federal Theater Project in New York. He had two children, Willson and Benjamin, from a previous marriage and was handsome, restless, and enterprising. Stephanie was his fourth wife. (Her maiden name was Frey, and her given name was Ruth. The name Stephanie was bestowed upon her by a college classmate.) Stephanie was a fashion journalist before she joined the firm as well as a talented amateur chanteuse; she had style and grace – and great determination.[3]

Benjamin Barber describes his father and stepmother's initiatives in Lenox as follows:

> Phil and Stephanie started Music Inn, [and later] the Music Barn and the School of Jazz as partners, with Phil acting as the driving force and ambition, and Stephanie taking care of the managerial and administrative aspects as well as becoming the hostess and beating heart of these institutions. Both had immense charm and charisma, which were in no small part responsible for the success of the Barn and the School, since neither of them was a professional musician. Without them there could have been no School of Jazz. It was their dream that made it happen.[4]

Juanita Giuffre, who was at the Lenox School of Jazz for two or three years as a faculty wife, describes Stephanie Barber as "quite something – a real catalyst. There were no half measures with her."[5] The Barbers transformed the carriage house, stables, barn, icehouse, and other buildings ("a marvelous group of buildings")[6] on the site into an inn for travelers and vacationers, with "fishing, swimming, and boating . . . tennis, badminton, archery, table tennis, croquet and bicycling."[7] The buildings were all connected by stone walls, "like a little French village."[8] The grounds were covered with pines, birches, elms, maples and hemlocks, and boasted trails and a mile and a half of winding stream. There were accommodations for sixty-five guests.

The Barbers were cultural enthusiasts of broad tastes. They numbered among their friends the folklorist and singer Alan Lomax, poet Langston Hughes, composer Meredith Willson (who was Philip's first cousin and a close friend), and jazz scholar Marshall

The Barn at Music Inn in the early Fifties.

Stearns. From the very beginning they decided to make the inn a site for music making and musical investigation, with particular focus on folk music and jazz. (In an interview published in the 1958 program booklet for their summer music festival, the Barbers described Berkshire County as "the most pleasant place to live a civilized life in the United States." They said that they established the Inn because they "needed to make a living" and that they were "crazy about jazz.")[9] Stephanie recalled that opening the Inn was a considerable challenge. "People couldn't believe what we were doing. We opened an inn knowing absolutely nothing about it." She

herself was "a city girl . . . never having cooked, never having done anything. I didn't know how to boil an egg." But her husband was very enthused about the project. "He found the same vitality now in jazz as he had found in theater in the Thirties. . . . The jazz groups . . . were exploring, they were doing all kinds of things."[10] In general Philip would come on weekends and give instructions, and Stephanie would spend the whole week carrying them out. She later recalled: "Philip appeared every weekend. Everybody was so interested to know who my husband might be, since he was never around. Here was this handsome man, dressed beautifully, who would appear on weekends, looking like the Duke of Wheatleigh, being charming. Everybody adored him, and then he made lots of directions for us to follow."[11]

Early Symposiums, "Roundtables," and Tanglewood

In the very first summer of operation of the Music Inn, Alan Lomax, the folk music archivist and performer, was scheduled to give a series of concerts and present items from his own collection of rare recordings. Woody Guthrie and Pete Seeger also performed. A symposium on the origins of jazz was organized, run by the jazz critic and author Marshall Stearns, who was also a professor of medieval English at New York University. It included African drummer Asadota Dafora, calypso singer Macbeth the Great, pianist and blues singer Dan Burley, and the Mura Dehn Dancers. A second week-long symposium on ragtime was held towards the end of the summer, featuring jazz writer Rudi Blesh; pianist Eubie Blake, who was then sixty-eight; singers Lillyn Brown and Edith Wilson; Johnny Mohegan, jazz instructor at the Juilliard School of Music; and dancers Leon James and Al Mins. A reporter for the *Berkshire Evening Eagle* wrote that the symposium, with its lectures and concerts, was "an extremely refreshing experience."

It is the first time that I have been able to hear one of my favorite types of music without being blinded and choked by cigarette smoke, without somebody's elbow being crowded into my large and sensitive nose, and without a waiter pushing expensive, watered drinks down my throat every 37 seconds. Stephanie and Philip Barber, owners of the resort, are to be commended for importing such a treat to Berkshire County. [1]

The Music Inn was down the road from Tanglewood, which was fast becoming one of the most important summer venues for classical music in the country. The opening of the Music Inn coincided with the Tanglewood debut of Charles Munch, the new music director of the Boston Symphony. (Long-time and legendary director Serge Koussevitsky had died earlier that year.) Some of the teachers and students at Tanglewood could be found at the Music Inn during their off hours. In attendance at the concert reviewed in the *Berkshire Evening Eagle* was a former student of Tanglewood, who in 1951 was head of their conducting and orchestral departments, Leonard Bernstein. The American composer Marc Blitzstein was also there. According to Stephanie Barber, the distinguished composer Aaron Copland, who was head of the teaching faculty at Tanglewood, used to come by as well.[2] Since students from Tanglewood were housed at the main Heredia mansion nearby, they too began dropping in to Music Inn in the evenings "for impromptu concerts and chatter by the fire," according to a local gossip column.[3] A second symposium on "Definitions in Jazz" was held later in the summer, featuring "experts in the fields of anthropology, sociology, musicology, folklore, and psychology" as well as "top-notch jazzmen."[4]

Gospel singer Mahalia Jackson was invited to be a part of the discussions that summer. She was interviewed by the critics and professors about the jazz elements in gospel. ("She was going to stay two days, but it really ended up being more like two weeks," said Stephanie.)[5] She dispelled their misconceptions. "Now I hear a lot of [talk], like it's half jazz. Well, gospel isn't! The way I see it, if you sing the gospel, you never need any artificial *anything*. . . ."[6] Marshall Stearns was enraptured by her singing. He wrote in his diary: "She breaks every rule of concert singing, taking breaths in the middle of a word, and sometimes garbling the words together. But the full-throated feeling and expression are seraphic!"[7] Mahalia Jackson and Stephanie Barber struck up a friendship that lasted for many years. Stephanie remembered years later that she had taken Mahalia to a concert at Tanglewood. Mahalia was overwhelmed and said, "I'm never going to sing again, never. Those are real musicians." But afterward Stephanie took her backstage and Leonard Bernstein, Aaron Copland, and Mrs. Koussevitsky were there and said how much they loved her singing and asked for her autograph.[8] Many years later, in a 1969 concert from the stage of Tanglewood, Mahalia Jackson reminisced about her first visit to the Music Inn. "And first thing I knew, these professors started comin' around' analyzin' me. I'd get outa bed in the mornin', there'd be a professor standin' there sayin', 'How'd she do that? How she sing that way?' Analyzin' me. Stephanie, she could see they was makin' me nervous, but I kept on singing for her and Phil and the folks there 'cause I knew they appreciated me. . . . Phil and Stephanie, they appreciated me, and when I left that little place, I missed 'em so."[9] Jackson stayed in fact for a week, singing in the lounge every night. Philip Barber recalled that she sang "so movingly that, had she wished, she surely could have led us all down into Stockbridge Bowl [the local lake] to be baptized."[10]

These weeklong "Roundtables" always included a central educational component along with performances. Marshall Stearns

*Marshall Stearns
in his New York City
apartment in 1954.*

acted as "master of ceremonies," as he began to be called in 1952.[11] Stearns taught a jazz course at New York University, and in 1952 he founded the Institute of Jazz Studies in New York, initially as a place to make available his extraordinary collection of (12,000!) recordings, as well as books, periodicals, sheet music, photographs, clipping files and memorabilia to writers and researchers on jazz. It was housed in his apartment, and featured a board of advisors that included Louis Armstrong, Dave Brubeck, Duke Ellington, Ralph Ellison, Leonard Feather, Norman Ganz, Langston Hughes, Stan Kenton, Curt Sachs, Artie Shaw, and Clarence Williams. But he continued to run the roundtables at the music Inn. In 1952 Stearns was named by the *Record Changer* magazine as "the critic who has done the most for jazz during the past ten years."[12] Speakers at the Roundtables in those early summers at Music Inn included professors, musicologists, a psychiatrist, painters, drummers, dancers, and pianists. Among this eclectic group of contributors were Willis James, professor at Spellman College and an expert in field cries of the South and the origins of spirituals and other African songs; psychiatrist Dr. Maurice Green; poet Sterling Brown, who was on the faculty of Howard University; drummer Dennis Strong, blues singer John Lee Hooker; dancer Mura Dehn; artist Bruce Mitchell; pianists Billy Taylor, Dick Katz, and Bob Greene; trumpeter Rex Stewart (who played in the Ellington band); blues players Sonny Terry and Brownie McGhee; folksinger and songwriter Tom Glaser; and clarinetist Tony Scott. Among the lecture topics were the connection between jazz and sex, jazz and popular culture, the blues, spirituals, and field hollers.

Benjamin Barber, who was eleven years old when his parents founded the Music Inn, remembers the excitement of the Roundtables: "I relished the historical discussions tracing musical modes and rhythms back to the Caribbean and Africa. Marshall Stearns, Nat Hentoff, John Lewis, Dave Brubeck, Paul Desmond, and especially Willis James were among the most articulate speakers, but the most surprising things sometimes came from the less voluble -- Connie Kay or Milt Jackson or Mahalia Jackson making a subtle point in a reticent but impressive fashion. Jimmy Giuffre was one of the gentlest and most thoughtful."[13] Benjamin and his older brother spent all the summers of their teenage years working very hard at the Inn, waiting tables, working in the kitchen, and helping with the jazz concerts.

The proximity to Tanglewood led to several comments on the juxtaposition of jazz and "serious" music. One elementary school teacher reported on her two-week stay in the Berkshires, and, in the distinctive vocabulary of the Fifties, wrote about her experiences as "ecstatic hepcats stalked the sacred sanctuary of the Long

Hair at Tanglewood, Mass." Although the Tanglewood season was in full sway, "somewhere at Music Inn lurked the echoes of a mad off-beat and the secret cry of blues in the night!"[14] Benjamin Barber remembers that "the Tanglewood management tried to shut down the Music Inn on Tanglewood concert nights when the two traditions of sound would collide over Lake Mahkeenac."[15] It is difficult to imagine today, in the era of a nationwide veneration of jazz, established jazz festivals, and the imposing surroundings of Jazz at Lincoln Center, how startling it must have been for people in the 1950s to witness the encroachment of unrestrained jazz into the very heart of the hallowed precincts of classical music. This was still a time when bare legs were not permitted at Tanglewood, ushers wore white only (for the women) or jackets and ties (for the men) and handed out wraps for female audience members wearing shorts or slacks, and a newspaper editor wrote of the basic atmosphere of the Berkshires, "which is dignified and which ultimately imposes dignity on those who visit there."[16] Lenox itself was "famed internationally as a summer resort area for the very rich and the very exclusive."[17] Newspaper articles and headlines continued to point out the opposition between "longhair" music and jazz. "Tanglewood, Longhair Retreat, Enjoys a Scholarly Ragtime Invasion," announced one.[18] Another spoke of the entrance of jazz into the "stronghold of the three Bs."[19] And an article headlined "Ragtime Rival for Classics at Tanglewood" mentioned the reverberation of ragtime through "the pure classical air around Tanglewood."[20] "Sacrilege!" shouted another.[21]

Marshall Stearns defended the Inn in the pages of the *New York Times*: "The current activities at Music Inn, under the impressive shadow of Tanglewood and the Boston Symphony, enlarge and complete the picture of musical America."[22] The *Boston Globe* spoke of "the meeting of Brahms and Basie – a family reunion."[23]

The mingling of the two musical traditions was emblematic of the gradual breakdown of class barriers in postwar America. Gradually even exclusive Lenox was turning into a cultural center for the middle class as well. As Benjamin Barber, who is a political theorist, puts it, "This was an era when the summer playland of the rich became a rich cultural playground for middle America."[24]

Philip and Stephanie Barber's efforts – the obstacles they encountered as well as the success they achieved – were a reflection of the cultural and political climate of the Fifties. Stephanie Barber, who ran the Inn while her husband commuted to his business in New York during the week, was determined to create a place where the focus was on music and not on race or politics. At a time when African Americans could not find a room in many hotels and restaurants around the country, when black musicians often had to enter an establishment through the kitchens, and when "[i]n Lenox and Stockbridge . . . strong anti-Negro attitudes prevail[ed], despite the cultural surroundings," the Music Inn housed its black and white patrons and musicians side by side.[25] "Black people were not popular in New England," Stephanie Barber said. "[W]e had problems finding beds at local inns for artists who happened to be black. People in the village did not approve of what we were doing."[26] "Everybody was sort of in a state of shock that we had black people in our house staying with us under our roof."[27] As Benjamin Barber recalls, "The presence of so many black musicians, many with urban habits, had to be startling to the community – but no more startling than the open skies, woodlands, and rural landscapes were to the artists. An inn with a handful of black musicians was not a threatening presence to the community at large – more of a curiosity."[28] (In the Fifties Jews were also not welcome at almost all of the rural inns and hotels of America. The advertisements for these establishments used to include the phrase "Churches Nearby,"

Chapter Two

Dizzy Gillespie with a student at The Lenox School of Jazz.

which was code for "No Jews Allowed.") One of the earliest guests at the Music Inn was the distinguished African-American artist Jacob Lawrence. In the Barbers' art collection is a watercolor Lawrence made of the barn on the grounds of Music Inn.

Musicians at the Newport Jazz Festival still experienced bias four years after its founding. One of the Newport hotels still refused to accept black patrons, and accommodations in private homes were suddenly withdrawn when the owners discovered their guests were black.[29] Stephanie Barber did not tolerate political discrimination any more than she did racial discrimination. When a New York Times photographer tried to eliminate folk singer Pete Seeger from a group photo at the Music Inn because he was regarded as a communist, Barber simply said, "He stays in the shot or there is no picture."[30]

Flourishing of the Inn and the First "Jazz Festival"

By 1953 the Inn was open at holiday times as well as in the summer. A note in the United Nations internal newsletter *Secretariat News* mentions that twenty to twenty-five places were being reserved for UN staff members at the Music Inn for Christmas vacation, featuring "French cuisine, informal musicales, skating, skiing, sleighing, Buche de Noel [sic]."[1] Word was also spreading about its summer activities. The summer's events included appearances by the great blues singer Jimmy Rushing, the American cabaret singer Keith Lawrence, who specialized in French popular songs, and Cuban conga drummer Candido, and featured roundtables on the blues, swing, boogie-woogie, and "modern Bop."[2] Observers continued to note the proximity of Tanglewood and the Music Inn. According to Benjamin Barber, "Musicians went back and forth between Tanglewood and Music Inn,"[3] and others in Lenox remember quite a lot of interchange between the two groups. One resident recalls that "after concerts they used to get together in [anonymous, one of the violinists from the Boston Symphony Orchestra]'s house and jam."[4] One journalist took particular note of the daily commute of Leonard Bernstein, ("who has long labored to break down the phoney [sic] barriers between long- and short-hair music,") between his performances at Tanglewood and the jazz roundtable at Music Inn.[5]

At the Inn a reporter from *Business Week* happened upon a beautiful young woman strumming a guitar and singing love songs to a handsome young man. He later found out that the young woman was Felicia Montealegre and the handsome man her new husband, Leonard Bernstein.[6] The reporter's visit resulted in a three-page spread on the Music Inn in *Business Week* for September 19, 1953, a week in which the Dow Jones Industrial Average reached the dizzying height of 290.[7] The piece is lavishly illustrated with nearly twenty photographs of mostly informal music making by the guests at the Inn. Pictured are men and women, young and old, mostly white but some black, playing all kinds of instruments: piano, guitars (several), violin, recorder, steel drums, and, in one case, a comb. Bernstein and his wife are photographed with their musical roles reversed. She is now listening to him play the guitar and sing, while he entertains a group of listeners (including Stephanie Barber) with what the magazine identifies as "Arabian folk songs."[8] The photographs stress the joy of amateur music making, identifying three of the participants as "a New Orleans surgeon, a TV writer, and a college student."[9] The accompanying text, as might be expected for a magazine entitled *Business Week*, focuses on commercial considerations, including the success of Music Inn itself. "This year, Music Inn has seen 20% more business than last year. Rated at 100-guest capacity, the place often managed to put up 110 music hobbyists for a night."[10] The article points out that the

Music Inn was thriving because it catered to people who wanted to make music and not just listen to it. "There's a growing number of such people, and businesses are profiting from the trend. Makers and distributors of musical instruments are having a banner year. . . . [M]usic stores are selling more instruments than ever before." The article notes that the sheet music trade was declining, presumably because of the rapid rise of the recording industry.

The Music Inn was recommended as a place to stay in *Cue* magazine. "For the New Yorker who fancies himself a sophisticate," wrote the magazine, "the Music Inn is ideal."[11] Word about the Music Inn had even reached Louis Armstrong by 1953. In an interview in the *Springfield* [Massachusetts] *Sunday Republican*, Armstrong was asked about the jazz seminars held in Lenox every summer. "They're doing wonderful things for jazz up there," he said. "They're really helping make music history."[12] And he said that he himself would like to play there one day.

In May of 1954, the *New York Herald Tribune* featured a full-length article on Marshall Stearns and his "double life" as English scholar and jazz scholar. As in the long-hair/short-hair contrast often referred to in the juxtaposition of Tanglewood and the Music Inn, the subtext of the article is the highbrow nature of Chaucer and the lowbrow nature of jazz. "People always ask me," said Stearns," "'What's a Chaucer man doing fooling around with jazz?' They seem to think it's a joke. Well it isn't. Chaucer and jazz are quite similar: they both swing, they both have the same punch, vitality and guts. Why, they're not far apart at all."[13] (Stearns even used to compare Bessie Smith with the Wife of Bath.)[14]

The 1954 music season at Music Inn lasted for three weeks and was now dubbed a "Jazz Festival." The program was ambitious indeed, encompassing a variety of music under the heading "Folk and Jazz Roundtable," and featuring professors of music, history, folk culture, and semantics; composer Henry Cowell; poet Langston Hughes; jazz writers Rudi Blesh and Nat Hentoff; and performers Eubie Blake, Noble Sissle, Pete Seeger, Sonny Terry and Brownie McGhee, Billy Taylor, Jimmy Rushing, and Mama Yancey. The music ranged from blues to New Orleans marching bands to square dances, Jamaican music, the music and dance of Trinidad, and a "Calypso Costume Ball."

It should be noted that while the jazz festival is now a widespread international phenomenon, it was a new idea in the Fifties. The first important jazz festival in the United States was in Newport, and its first year was the same summer as that in Lenox, 1954. It represented an important change in the reception of jazz among American audiences, for the music was no longer regarded as the background to some other activity but as a kind of concert music to which focused attention should be paid.

Rate card for the Music Inn, 1955.

season rates 1955			room*	dorm*
Memorial Day weekend	special 3 day weekend May 27 to May 30		$42	$34
May 30 to June 6	graduation week: dinner, overnight, breakfast	$10		
June 6 to June 30	designed for honeymooners and travellers overnight and breakfast (in bed if you prefer)	$7		
July 4th weekend	special 3 day weekend July 1 to July 4		$45	$37
July 4 to July 10, 6 day week	single rooms		$81	
	rooms for 2		$73, $76, $79, $81, $83, $88	$63
	rooms for 3		$71, $76, $79, $81	
July 10 to August 14, weekly	single rooms		$91	
	rooms for 2		$83, $86, $89, $91, $93, $98	$73
	rooms for 3		$81, $86, $89, $91	
August 14 to August 28, weekly	single rooms		$81	
	rooms for 2		$73, $76, $79, $81, $83, $88	$63
	rooms for 3		$71, $76, $79, $81	
Labor Day week 8 days, August 28 to September 5	single room		$91	
	rooms for 2		$83, $86, $89, $91, $93, $98	$73
	rooms for 3		$81, $86, $89, $91	
Labor Day weekend	special 3 day weekend Sept. 2 to Sept. 5		$45	$37
September 5 to September 26	weekly		$60, $61, $62, $67, $68, $69	$57
	daily		$11	$9

*rate per person

Berkshire Music Festival at Tanglewood

Folk Song and Jazz Festivals at Music Inn

Extra days beyond one week (to Thursday) prorated at weekly rate.

Although preference is given to week-long reservations during July and August, weekend space sometimes does become available.
If so, there is a 2-day minimum on reserved weekend space — $32 per person in the rooms and $26 in the dorms.
For weekend reservations, phone us at Lenox 695 the preceding Tuesday.

about the variations in rate:
We believe all accommodations will please you, but naturally the rooms vary somewhat in desirability. We have found that room preferences are largely a matter of personal taste, with guests sometimes definitely preferring a less expensive room. In general, location, size, and number of occupants, as well as bath, determine the rate.

American plan
3 meals a day

The Music Barn and the First Summer Series of Jazz Concerts in the U.S.

In the summer of 1955, the Lenox property blossomed into a major American venue for the presentation of jazz. The Barbers expanded their season by an extra five weeks and converted a large barn adjoining the Inn into a new (partly outdoor) performing space for music with seating for 750. "The only jobs [jazz] musicians could get then," said Stephanie Barber, "were in cellars or nightclubs full of smoke and lots of talk, where they got paid very little. We thought it would be marvelous for them to have a concert hall where they could present their music – their own Carnegie Hall."[1] Keeping the Roundtable on jazz and folk music to the three weeks (mid-August to early September) after the Tanglewood season ended, they put in place a five-week Jazz Festival that overlapped with the Tanglewood season and ran from early July to mid August. Calling the new venue The Music Barn only made the parallel with Tanglewood more obvious, for the Boston Symphony Orchestra played at Tanglewood in a large open-sided building known as The Shed. The

1955 concert series at the Music Barn was the first summer series of jazz concerts in the United States.

The establishment of the Music Barn (and the comparison with Tanglewood) did not sit well with many local people. "When we opened the Music Barn," said Stephanie Barber, "there was a to-do like you can't believe. They were outraged! How could we have a jazz barn down the road from the Tanglewood concerts?"[2]

However the importance of the Barbers' establishment started to attract major figures in the jazz world; the offerings at the Music Barn began to be listed alongside those of Tanglewood, Jacob's Pillow, and the local theater festivals; and word spread around the country. Playing in the festival at the Music Barn in 1955 was a remarkable array of distinguished performers. They included trumpeters Art Farmer, Dizzy Gillespie, and Bobby Hackett, veteran tenor saxophonist Coleman Hawkins, Count Basie with a seventeen-piece band, the Max Roach-Clifford Brown ensemble, the recently formed Modern Jazz Quartet, the Dave Brubeck Quartet, drummer Gene Krupa with his combo, singer Jimmy Rushing, bop pianist Thelonious Monk, saxophonist Lucky Thompson, bandleader Eddie Condon, and vibraphonist Teddy Charles (in a quartet that included bassist Charles Mingus). Savoy dancers Al Minns and Leon James were frequent guests at many of these concerts. This list is notable not only for its length but also for its breadth. The players range from purveyors of the hot style of the Twenties and Swing music of the Thirties and Forties to exponents of the newest styles in modern jazz. Since they had broad musical tastes, the Barbers also showcased the flamenco guitarist Carlos Montoya, folksinger Richard Dyer-Bennet, unconventional blind percussionist Moondog, the folk group The Wayfarers, and gospel singer Ernestine Washington.[3]

A ten-page professional brochure was printed up for the Music Barn (official name Berkshire Music Barn), with comments by

*Events flyer for the
Berkshire Music Barn,
1955.*

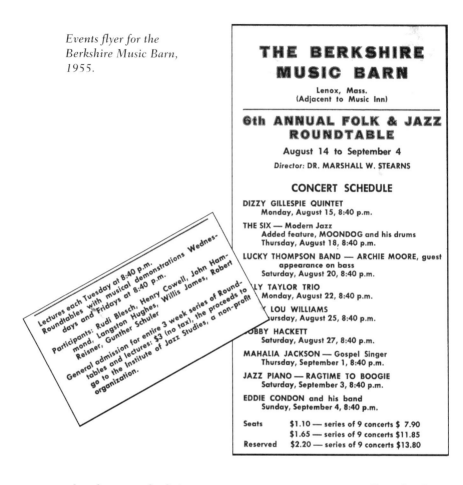

**THE BERKSHIRE
MUSIC BARN**

Lenox, Mass.
(Adjacent to Music Inn)

**6th ANNUAL FOLK & JAZZ
ROUNDTABLE**

August 14 to September 4
Director: DR. MARSHALL W. STEARNS

CONCERT SCHEDULE

DIZZY GILLESPIE QUINTET
Monday, August 15, 8:40 p.m.

THE SIX — Modern Jazz
Added feature, MOONDOG and his drums
Thursday, August 18, 8:40 p.m.

LUCKY THOMPSON BAND — ARCHIE MOORE, guest
appearance on bass
Saturday, August 20, 8:40 p.m.

…LY TAYLOR TRIO
Monday, August 22, 8:40 p.m.

… LOU WILLIAMS
…ursday, August 25, 8:40 p.m.

…BBY HACKETT
Saturday, August 27, 8:40 p.m.

MAHALIA JACKSON — Gospel Singer
Thursday, September 1, 8:40 p.m.

JAZZ PIANO — RAGTIME TO BOOGIE
Saturday, September 3, 8:40 p.m.

EDDIE CONDON and his band
Sunday, September 4, 8:40 p.m.

Seats $1.10 — series of 9 concerts $ 7.90
             $1.65 — series of 9 concerts $11.85
Reserved $2.20 — series of 9 concerts $13.80

Lectures each Tuesday at 8:40 p.m. with musical demonstrations Wednesdays and Fridays at 8:40 p.m. Roundtables Participants: Rudi Blesch, Henry Cowell, John Hammond, Langston Hughes, Willis James, Robert Reisner, Gunther Schuler General admission for entire 3 week series of Roundtables and lectures: $3 (no tax), the proceeds to go to the Institute of Jazz Studies, a non-profit organization.

the distinguished American composer Henry Cowell and others, including jazz critic Nat Hentoff; notes on some of the performers; and, of course, advertisements, including one for "The Most Fabulous Jazz Record Ever Released!," a 12-inch Columbia LP for 98 cents.[4] Cowell joined authors Rudi Blesh and Robert Reisner (who was managing the Barn that summer) and Professor of Semantics S. I. Hayakawa in attempting a textbook definition of jazz.[5] These scholarly musings stood next to Louis Armstrong's famous statement: "What's jazz? Man, if you don't know by now – don't mess with it!" Newspapers further afield started carrying articles about the jazz festival and the folk and jazz roundtable. In the summer and fall of 1955 the Music Barn or Music Inn is mentioned in the Springfield (Massachusetts) *Morning Union*; the Fall River, Massachusetts, *Herald News*; the North Adams, Massachusetts, *Transcript*; the Holyoke, Massachusetts, *Transcript-Telegram*; the *Boston Globe*; the *Boston Herald*; the Chatham, New York, *Courier*; the Albany, New York, *Knickerbocker News*; the Schenectady, New York, *Gazette*; the *New Yorker*; the *New York Times*; the New York *Daily News*; the New York *Herald Tribune*; the Hackensack, New Jersey, *Bergen Record*; the Asbury Park, New Jersey, *Press*; the New Brunswick, New Jersey, *Home News*; the Morristown, New Jersey, *Record*; the New Haven, Connecticut, *Register*; the New Britain, Connecticut, *Herald*; as well as the music magazine *Down Beat*. Articles also appeared in newspapers as far away as Easton, Pennsylvania; Charlotte, North Carolina; Dayton, Ohio; Toledo, Ohio; St. Paul, Minnesota; Sioux Falls, South Dakota; and San Diego, California. The *New York Times* described the Music Barn as a "complementary enterprise" to the Newport Jazz Festival and said "the audience for authentic jazz is enormous."[6] In *Down Beat* Nat Hentoff described the Music Barn as "the first 'summer home' for jazz."[7] *Metronome* drew its readers' attention to "something very exciting going on in Lenox."[8]

Stephanie Barber's role as the enterprising woman who ran both the Inn and the Music Barn was noted by several writers for the "women's pages" of contemporary newspapers. Under one article's headline "Blonde Converts Barn to Profit," Stephanie Barber's hard work and business acumen are praised along with her "sultry blonde" looks.[9] "Neighbors now remark thoughtfully that one really never should underestimate the power of a woman," reports the

41

article, while describing her husband's admiration for her work:

> Phil, tho [sic] a little dazed by the changes wrought in his life by his wife, is filled with nothing but admiration for her. Having taught drama at Yale for six years, he likes having a country theater of his own. He also likes having an inn-keeping wife, who can attract the country's top jazz artists to their little establishment. He likes best, perhaps, the fact that she is able to show a profit on her enterprises, and that despite her talent for hard work and business acumen she continues to look like a glamour girl.

The "glamour girl" aspect of Stephanie Barber's life was stressed, along with her business acumen, in a fashion photo in the *Berkshire Eagle* in September 1956.[10] She was shown posing at the Music Barn, dressed in a short-sleeved tunic and tights. The tunic was made for her by a guest and is appliquéd with the Barn's distinctive weathervane and trimmed with sequins. But the spread, which featured the personnel director of a large department store and the executive secretary of a community service organization in addition to Stephanie Barber, focused on the working lives of the women pictured as well as their clothes. While she freely admitted that she loved "costumey clothes," the article draws attention to Barber's roles as "impresario," "innkeeper," and "concert manager."

The brochures for the Music Inn for 1955 now show that the Inn was open from Memorial Day to the end of September and for the main holidays in the winters: from Christmas Eve to January 2; President Lincoln's Birthday weekend (February 11-13); and President Washington's Birthday four-day weekend (February 19-22). On view in the converted icehouse building where the Barbers lived (the "Nice House," as the Barbers called it) was the Barbers' large private collection of French posters from the 1890s, including works by Cheret, Toulouse-Lautrec, Guillaume, Bonnard, Grun, Bouisset, and Roubille. The lounge also featured a remarkable sound panel designed by the chief of electronics of the Chrysler Corporation, made up of 108 six-inch speakers.[11] Room rates ranged from $63 to $91 a week.

THE BOSTON HERALD, THURSDAY, APRIL 28, 1955

Music from Bop to Brahms at Lenox

Tanglewood Gets Jazz Barn Almost Next to Symphony

NEW YORK, April 27 (AP)—The Berkshire Music Barn, devoted to jazz music of the modern, or bop, variety, will open this summer at Lenox, Mass., just down the road from the Boston Symphony's Music Shed.

Top: Headline announcing the opening of the Music Barn.

Right: Stephanie Barber, the "Glamour Girl."

Chapter 7

1956: Enlargement of the Barn,
The Modern Jazz Quartet
in Residence,
Two Recordings from the Inn

In 1956 Louis Armstrong's wish of three years earlier was fulfilled. He played the opening night of the Music Barn season in front of what the local newspaper described as an "enthusiastic, overflow audience" of over one thousand people.[1] The *Tanglewood Times* of 1957 carried a delightful photograph of Armstrong and Stephanie Barber sharing a quiet moment and a Coke together.

Stephanie later told the story of how they had managed to get the Armstrong booking:

> Getting Louis Armstrong is a story in itself. Getting him from that awful man, Joe Glaser [Armstrong's manager]. I will never forget that interview with Glaser . . . When I came in, he screamed at me, "Sit down over there!" He never stopped sitting on envelopes to close them. He did his own mail addressing and closing, so he would

Stephanie Barber enjoying a moment of relaxation with Louis Armstrong.

write it, lick it, and sit on it. All during the entire interview, that's what happened. It made me a little bit nervous. He said, "You want Louis Armstrong to play on some mountain that I can't even pronounce the name of? Are you crazy? . . . [Y]ou have the nerve to want him to come up to a place I've never heard of." So I said, "Well, I'm sorry." He was still sitting on the envelopes, and I went to the door. I don't know what made me stop. I turned around at the door. I had nothing to lose, I figured. I said, "Mr. Glaser, do you and Louis need money so much that you cannot take a chance on a very exciting new way to present jazz . . . ? You really need money that much? Still sitting on his stamps, he said, "When do you want him?". . . I just floated out of there.[2]

Concert-goers approach the Music Barn with its striped awning.

The Barbers kept expanding the features (and the size) of their "little establishment" in Lenox. A striped canvas roof was installed over the outdoor area, and seating capacity was enlarged from 750 to 900.[3] (The additional Armstrong enthusiasts must have sat on the grass.) The music festival was now called the Jazz and Folk Festival, with jazz concerts on Sunday nights, folk concerts on Saturday afternoons, and a special Thursday night series entitled "Concerts for Connoisseurs," which presented stars of "modern jazz." (These nights were chosen to avoid clashes with Tanglewood concerts, which were scheduled on Friday and Saturday nights and Sunday afternoons.) In addition, the Modern Jazz Quartet was now "in residence" at the Music Inn, working together and with other musicians on their music and on "experiments in jazz."[4] The group had been formed four years earlier, but 1956 was a breakthrough year. They played at Newport and traveled to Europe and were becoming known as a first-class jazz combo. By the end of the decade the Modern Jazz Quartet was renowned worldwide. The idea of having the members of the MJQ in residence at the Inn came simultaneously to Philip Barber and John Lewis, the group's leader. Stephanie Barber recalled: "One day Phil said, 'You know, I have an idea.' And John Lewis said to him: 'I accept!' It was incredible."[5]

The members of the MJQ very much appreciated the opportunity to be in the country for a few weeks, away from the pressures of their touring and of the city. June Heath, bassist Percy Heath's wife, who accompanied him to Lenox every summer, says, "It was just wonderful to be in the mountains." Her oldest son, then four years old, "ran around helping everyone." And she continued, "I have wonderful memories – getting the chance to meet our contemporaries, Mahalia Jackson and Langston Hughes – and Percy loved to teach the young people coming up."[6]

Concerts were supplemented by "[d]aily lectures, round table discussions and demonstrations by jazz and folk critics, historians and musicians."[7] And the late-summer Folk and Jazz Roundtable, still organized by Marshall Stearns, continued into its sixth year. It was in 1956 that Marshall Stearns published *The Story of Jazz*, a book that he had written under a Guggenheim Fellowship and that became a widely used historical survey of the music.[8] That same year the State Department sent Stearns with Dizzy Gillespie and his band on a trip to Eastern Europe, the Middle East, and Asia. The band played, and Stearns spoke on the history and significance of American jazz.[9]

Armstrong's opening concert put the gloss on another season that featured some of the biggest names in jazz: Count Basie, Duke Ellington, Tommy and Jimmy Dorsey, Erroll Garner, Sarah Vaughan, Dizzy Gillespie, and the Glen Miller Band in the Sunday night series; Lee Konitz, Bud Powell, Stan Getz, Shelly Manne, J. J. Johnson, Tony Scott, Phineas Newborn, Chico Hamilton, Marian McPartland, Max Roach, and Kai Winding in the Thursday night "Concerts for Connoisseurs."[10] The program booklet contained notes on some of the performers as well as advertisements for record companies, "hi-fi" systems, *Down Beat* magazine, the new *Encyclopedia of Jazz*, and Armstrong's memoirs, *Satchmo: My Life in New Orleans*.[11] There were also ads for some establishments one can still find today in the town of Lenox or nearby: the Curtis Hotel (now an apartment building), Wheeler and Taylor Real Estate, Carr Hardware, Loeb's grocery store, and the famous Red Lion Inn. At the beginning of the season, the Music Barn was featured in the *New York Times* in a countrywide list of 38 prominent music venues that included the Lewisohn Stadium concerts in New York, the Ravinia Festival in Chicago, the Aspen Festival in Colorado, and the Hollywood Bowl concerts in California.[12]

The residency of the Modern Jazz Quartet and other musicians at the Music Inn was sponsored by the Barbers and dubbed a jazz "colony" on the analogy of the MacDowell colony in Peterborough, New Hampshire, which was founded in 1907 and offers room, board, and a congenial working environment for writers, composers, and other creative artists. The association of the MJQ and its leader, John Lewis, with the Music Inn was to last until the end of the decade and would prove musically and intellectually productive as well as personally satisfying. (Stephanie recalled: "We met John Lewis of the Modern Jazz Quartet, and there was always . . . a very keen affinity between us.")[13]

The first tangible results of the residency were two recordings, *The Modern Jazz Quartet at Music Inn, Guest Artist: Jimmy Giuffre* (Atlantic 1247), recorded August 28, 1956, and *Historic Jazz Concert at Music Inn* (Atlantic 1298) recorded August 30, 1956, both recorded at the Inn in Lenox. The former is a fine album, now available on CD (but only as a Japanese import),[14] with superb collaboration between the quartet and the reedman. Giuffre was one of the principal figures of the West Coast "cool" school and a sophisticated composer and performer of modern jazz. He had a distinctive breathy tone on clarinet and favored the instrument's lower register. He became very active at the Music Inn and at the School of Jazz, and he and his wife ultimately made their home in the Berkshires, where they still live. "There was no other place like it," said Giuffre. "It's why I moved up here."[15] The album contains one of the first compositions dedicated directly to the Barbers' special musical venue in the Berkshires: John Lewis's "Fugue for Music Inn," which should be added to the list of Lewis's fugal compositions that includes "Vendome," "Versailles," and "Concorde." The other tracks with Giuffre are David Raksin's slow, classical "Serenade" and Giuffre's own "Fun," which is simultaneously perky and serious. (Raksin was a film composer who wrote the extremely popular theme for the 1944 film *Laura*. "Serenade" was composed for the 1953 United Productions of America animated film of James Thurber's *The Unicorn in the Garden*.) On all these tracks the breathy clarinet provides a perfect foil to Lewis's spare piano style and especially to Milt Jackson's pealing vibraphone. Also on the album are the MJQ's versions of Gershwin's "Oh, Bess, Oh Where's My Bess," Harold Arlen's "The Man That Got Away," and performances of Lewis's "Two Degrees East, Three Degrees West," "Sun Dance," and "A Morning in Paris." The album concludes with Lewis's marvelous version of the traditional English carol "God Rest Ye, Merry Gentlemen," which the quartet also treats contrapuntally. The cover photo shows the five men in the middle of a field on the grounds of the Inn. John Wilson, critic for the *New York Times*, writes in the liner notes, "It's a long trip from dingy backroom dives in New Orleans to a sun-bathed, verdant hillside in the Berkshire Mountains of Massachusetts, but jazz has made the journey."[16]

Juanita Giuffre, Jimmy's wife, told me, "Jimmy loved his time at the Music Inn and the Lenox School of Jazz, where he could interact with young people from all over the world. Everything there was so well thought out and done so well. It was really top notch."[17]

The second recording of 1956 (*Historic Jazz Concert at Music Inn*) features Giuffre and Connie Kay, the drummer of the MJQ, together with other guests of the Inn, including flutist Herbie Mann, clarinetist Pee Wee Russell, cornetist Rex Stewart, vibraphonist Teddy Charles, bassists Oscar Pettiford and Ray Brown, and pianists Dick Katz and George Wein. Wein was the impresario who had founded the Newport Jazz Festival in 1954 and went on to found many more festivals for jazz, folk, and rock music around the world. Perhaps he was scouting for ideas as well as playing, for, as we shall see, later Newport Festivals reflected some important as-

Pee Wee Russell and Jimmy Giuffre, with Oscar Pettiford and Connie Kay, at the Music Inn, 1956.

pects of the Music Inn experience. The record only has four tracks, however – "Blues in E-flat," "In a Mellotone," "The Quiet Time," and "Body and Soul" – and was not released until three years later. It has long been out of print.[18] The track "Blues in E-flat" is an eleven-minute improvisation, pairing the young clarinetist Jimmy Giuffre with the veteran clarinetist Pee Wee Russell. A review drew attention to the collaboration as well as the contrast. "Giuffre is a clarinetist of dulcet restraint, Russell a man of droll, insinuating, spiral delicacy and sentiment. In duet, the two complement each other beautifully; in solo, each is superb."[19] It is amusing to hear Giuffre instructing pianist Wein in the course of the performance. After the opening Giuffre tells Wein: "Block chords!", and, before a stop time section the clarinetist demands: "Gimme a break!". These comments (together with the occasional "Good") as well as the audience sounds give the recording a delightful immediacy. Cornetist Rex Stewart reprises Duke Ellington's "In A Mellotone" with Giuffre on tenor sax. Wein acquits himself creditably on this tune (without instruction). "The Quiet Time" is a lyrical and gentle Giuffre tune, which was also recorded by the Teddy Charles Tentet.[20] "Body and Soul" features Herbie Mann on flute and Oscar Pettiford playing cello.

The liner notes to this record, written by Nat Hentoff, draw attention to the panel discussions held at the Music Inn at the end of August 1956. "For five days, a number of jazz musicians of widely varying ages and 'schools' were invited . . . to sit and discuss . . . specific jazz subjects." The main focus of the panels was improvisation, though topics also included "Composition and Instrumentation," "Rhythm," "Instrumental Tradition and the Development of Instrumental Techniques," and "Jazz and Its Audience: Communication." Among the panelists were Charles Mingus, Milt Jackson, Dick Katz, Jimmy Giuffre, John Lewis, Oscar Pettiford, Quincy Jones, Willie "The Lion" Smith, Ray Brown, Count Basie, Freddie Greene, Thad Jones, Connie Kay, Max Roach, Sonny Rollins, and Dizzy Gillespie. (Stephanie said that "Gillespie . . . turned out to be one of the best teachers that we ever had here."[21] Later Gillespie wrote that the atmosphere of the School was "creative and therapeutic. . . . [Charlie Parker] would have enjoyed it if he had lived.")[22] Some edited transcripts of these conversations were published in *Metronome*, *Jazz Today*, and *Down Beat* magazines.[23] And at the final concert of the summer, on September 2, 1956, John Lewis summed up the events of the previous few days:

> This past week has been one of the most exciting events . . . in the history of jazz. We have had panels of musicians, musicians talking to each other about their musical problems and making real communication. This kind of communication is very rare for us. We see each other very seldom, and when we do, we're generally crying on each other's shoulders, talking about no gigs and no money. But this week we talked about our music.[24]

John Lewis was clearly enthused about the experience, but he was also disturbed at how much of the valuable interchange would simply disappear, and he encouraged the Barbers to establish a more formal organization in which the accumulated wisdom of the participants might be passed on to others.[25] The result was the foundation of the seventh institution (after the Music Inn, the Roundtables, the Music Barn, the Jazz Festival, the Jazz and Folk Festival, and the residencies) on the Barbers' country property: an institution that was to take advantage of the immediate proximity of the Music Barn's jazz concerts, incorporate Marshall Stearns's roundtables, feature lectures on different aspects of jazz performance and reception, and offer instruction in composition and instrumental techniques: The Lenox School of Jazz.

The Opening of
the Lenox School of Jazz

The School opened in 1957, with a "small, carefully selected body of students," and it was established as a separate non-profit organization.[1] In the liner notes to *Historic Jazz Concert At Music Inn* Nat Hentoff writes that at the concert the "mutual affection and warmth [were] exhilaratingly contagious, and it was this experience that led directly to the decision by the Barbers and John Lewis to form the School of Jazz at Music Inn, where for the first time . . . young players could learn directly from the men who helped to form the jazz language."

The School had as its Executive Director, John Lewis; as its dean, pianist, artistic administrator, and agent Jules Foster (who also took over the management of the Music Barn); and Philip Barber, Stephanie Barber, Nesuhi Ertegun, J. J. Johnson, and Gunther Schuller were members of its Governing Committee. J. J. Johnson was an accomplished trombonist who could play both in the swing and the bop styles, but he also a skillful arranger and original composer. Gunther Schuller was an all-around musician, composer, and scholar. He played French horn in the Metropolitan Opera Orchestra and had taken part in the famous and influential jazz recordings with Miles Davis (1949-50) that were later dubbed *Birth of the Cool*. He and John Lewis were friends and colleagues. Together they had founded the Modern Jazz Society in 1955, which put on concerts in New York and elsewhere. Nesuhi Ertegun was the son of the Turkish ambassador to the United States. He and his brother Ahmet were jazz enthusiasts who ran the Atlantic record company, a company that became one of the most important jazz, rhythm-and-blues, and soul jazz labels in the country. It was because of his association with the School of Jazz that some of the historic performances at the School were captured on disc. Atlantic records also held a long-term contract with the Modern Jazz Quartet. Their first recording project together had been the Modern Jazz Quartet's *Fontessa* (1956; Atlantic 1231), which contains the marvelous four-movement Fontessa Suite as well as the fugue "Versailles."

Trustees of the School included jazz writers and scholars Bill Coss, Whitney Balliett, Leonard Feather, Nat Hentoff, André Hodeir, Willis James, Marshall Stearns, Jack Tracy, Barry Ulanov, and John Wilson. Most of these men were journalists and critics, though Stearns and James were also professors, and Hodeir was the author of the influential book *Jazz: Its Evolution and Essence*, which had been published a year before.[2] Other trustees were performers Dizzy Gillespie, Jimmy Giuffre, Wilbur DeParis, Oscar Peterson, Max Roach, and Bill Russo; German jazz enthusiast and producer Horst Lippman; and writer and producer for Columbia Records George Avakian. Within three years trustees' names included even more distinguished writers and performers such as Leonard Bernstein,

Dave Brubeck, Dorothy Fields, Ralph Gleason, John Hammond, Langston Hughes, Monte Kay, Artie Shaw, Frederick Steinway, and Martin Williams. Stephanie told of how, when they were forming the first board of trustees, Philip "had the great idea to have the meeting at the Harvard Club [in New York City.] . . . Almost everybody who was with us, I think, except a few like Philip and me and Marshall [Stearns] were black. Dizzy, as we were on the way to the dining room, stopped at the bar, and he said; 'Oh, you have a very nice selection [of liqueurs]. I'll have one of each and please send it into the next room.' . . . [T]he staff had never seen so many black people at once in their lives [or] Dizzy in his autocratic guise. That was simply marvelous."[3]

The School was incorporated as a non-profit organization, and its charter read, in part, as follows:

> The purpose of the School of Jazz, Inc., is to teach and to foster the study of jazz in all its aspects, including its techniques of expression, its improvisation and its composition; also its history, origin, its international development and its relationship to other arts; to provide for individual instruction as well as rehearsal in both large ensemble and in small groups, and to develop for its students the experience of playing for public audiences.

The School of Jazz that began operation in Lenox in 1957 under the directorship of John Lewis was perhaps the most significant of all the Barbers' initiatives at Music Inn. *Metronome* described the school as "the most important step taken in jazz."[4] "The School of Jazz was a groundbreaking experiment," said John Lewis many years later, "and although it lasted only a short time, its impact was felt far beyond the confines of Music Inn. The opportunity to form the School of Jazz was an incredible present from God, and I didn't ask any questions. . . . "[5] As we have seen, the number of well-known teachers – and students who ultimately became well-known – who passed through this small and relatively informal school in the Berkshire hills of western Massachusetts is quite remarkable.[6] The school was also one of the first places in the country to hire some of the most prominent performers in jazz to instruct young people in their musical art. Support also came from down the road, for music stands, blackboards, and other items were loaned to the School by Tanglewood.

In the first year, thirty-four young musicians were chosen by taped audition. They came from around the United States and abroad, and some were supported by scholarships. Their expertise was intended to be distributed fairly evenly among the instruments, but in the end nineteen of them turned out to be pianists.[7] Somehow small combos were formed and rehearsed their pieces with their coaches. The rehearsals were separated by lectures and by both professional and student concerts. The 1957 schedule included lectures on a wide variety of topics: "The Primitive Beginnings of Jazz," "Personalities in Jazz," "Jazz in Television," "The Music of Africa," "Jazz and Its Correlation to the Arts," "Techniques in Jazz Composition," "Management and Booking of Jazz," "Jazz Frontiers," "Problems in Jazz Recording," "New Directions in Jazz," "Jazz Frontiers," and "The Function of the Critic in Jazz." Among the lecturers were modern jazz pianist Lennie Tristano; Teo Macero, producer at Columbia Records; Ellington trumpeter Rex Stewart; *New York Times* critic John Wilson; composer/arranger for the Stan Kenton orchestra, Bill Russo; Marshall Stearns; and the Atlantic Records producer Nesuhi Ertegun. Professional concerts (at the Music Barn) were given by gospel singer Mahalia Jackson, trombonist Wilbur de Paris with his New Orleans revival band, and the Oscar Peterson Trio, with guests Dizzy Gillespie and Max Roach.

On Thursday, August 29, there was held a final concert by faculty and students. Based on the Tanglewood tradition of showcasing its faculty and students at a yearly extravaganza called "Tanglewood on Parade," this concert was entitled "School of Jazz on Parade." The rather lengthy program for this concert is reproduced here:

SCHOOL OF JAZZ

Concert by the Students and Faculty - August 29, 1957 at 8:40 P.M.

Small Ensemble, Oscar Peterson, Director

> Here Us Is [Bob Dorough]
> Jitney Jump [Bob Dorough]
> Little Red Riding Hood Minus the Wolf [Bob Flanik]
> 'Nough Said [Neil Hope]
> Here Us Was [Bob Dorough]

Dale Hillary-Alto Sax, Bob Wigton-Baritone Sax, Henry Ettman-Drums, Bob Dorough-Piano, Neil Hope-Piano, Bob Flanik-Piano, Ralph Pena-Bass

Small Ensemble, Dizzy Gillespie, Director

> Purple Sounds [Dizzy Gillespie]
> Housatonic Huzzy [Fran Thorne]
> Con Alma [Dizzy Gillespie]
> South Wales [Ron Riddle]
> Wheatleigh [Hall] [Dizzy Gillespie]

Connie Kay-Drums, Percy Heath-Bass, James Miltenberger-French Horn, John Mason-Trumpet, Fran Thorne-Piano, Ron Riddle-Piano

Small Ensemble, Ray Brown, Director

Ray Brown Blues [Ray Brown]
Applesauce [John Harmon]
Bellyroll Bows [Dave Blume]
Wende [Ran Blake]
Oh, My Gosh [Dexter Morrill]

Ray Brown-Bass, Terry Hawkeye-Drums, Dexter Morrill-Trumpet,
Kent McGarity-Trombone, John Harmon-Piano, Ran Blake-Piano,
Dave Blume-Piano

INTERMISSION

Small Ensemble, Jimmy Giuffre, Director

Blues for the Barn [Jimmy Giuffre]
Okeefeenokee Overture [Tupper Saussy]
Round Midnight [Thelonious Monk]
Rhythm Rears Its Head [Jimmy Giuffre]

Tom Scannell-Trumpet, John Thorpe-Trombone, Jimmy Giuffre-
Sax and Clarinet, Peter Denny-Vibes, Herb Ellis-Guitar, Margot
Pennell-Piano, Tupper Saussy-Piano, José Edward Homen de
Mello-Bass, Colin Cooke-Drums

Small Ensemble, Max Roach, Director

Cakle Hut [Owen Marshall]
Good Gravy [Teddy Edwards]
LaRue [Clifford Brown, arr. Paul Mowatt]
What is This Thing Called Love [Cole Porter]
Minor Trouble [Ray Bryant]

Pat Haggerty-Tenor Sax, John Conway-Vibes, Jim Hall-Guitar, Paul Mowatt-Piano, John McLean-Piano, Chuck Israels-Bass, Max Roach-Drums

INTERMISSION

Large Ensemble, Bill Russo, Director

Tickletoe [Lester Young]
Jig-Saw [Mulvihill, Baker, Galino, Mathieu]
Manteca [Dizzy Gillespie, arr. Bill Russo]
Pussy Willow [Bill Russo and Petan]
Picadilly Circus [Sture Swenson]

Saxophones: Dale Hillary, Pat Haggerty, Bob Wigton, Jimmy Giuffre, Bob Dorough. Trumpets: Dexter Morrill, John Mason, Tom Scannell, Dizzy Gillespie. Trombones: John Thorpe, Kent McGarity. Horn: Jim Miltenberger. Double Bass: Ray Brown. Guitar: Herb Ellis. Drums: Terry Hawkeye, Henry Ettman. Piano: Dave Blume, Fran Thorne, Tupper Saussy, and John Harmon.

The concert was "widely and wildly acclaimed by almost every one in attendance."[8] As we can see from the program, the new surroundings inspired new compositions for the concert: Fran Thorne's "Housatonic Huzzy," referring to the river that runs through the Berkshires, and Dizzy Gillespie's tribute to the mansion on the grounds: "Wheatleigh Hall." The program also shows that the pedagogical strategy of the School was to have the professionals play alongside the students in the combos and the big band.

The collegial nature of the school and the unique opportunities it offered were emphasized by faculty members and students alike. The director, John Lewis, said in an interview that was published that July:

No one is attending the school to be tested. Even if they couldn't play at all, they could gain something from the imaginative men who are doing the teaching. After all, we are most interested in the approach to jazz. [I]t is the approach that we will emphasize. We are trying to stimulate [the students'] imaginations, and any creative person will benefit from this.[9]

And after the summer had ended *Down Beat* reported that "[a]t Lenox, the School of Jazz showed that conscientious jazzmen who know their instruments, the working conditions of jazz, and who are intelligent and patient, can accomplish much in three short weeks to show the younger ones some of the paths to take and some of the pitfalls to avoid."[10]

We know too that both students and faculty were encouraged to take the school seriously. Lewis decreed that all students would be addressed as Mister or Miss regardless of their age and that all nine o'clock classes would begin at 9 a.m. regardless of the life-long habits of the faculty members. There would be no alcohol in student rooms or smoking in the practice rooms, and "the atmosphere should at all times represent its purposes of intensive, creative study." The curriculum involved classes in the mornings and afternoons, lectures in the evenings, and homework as well. Not mentioned, of course, are the informal discussions at breakfast, lunch, and dinner, or the music-making sessions that went on around the grounds constantly during the day and in the students' rooms into the night.[11]

A little of the working atmosphere of the school is provided by Ron Riddle, a piano student in the summer of 1957:

It was my particular good fortune to be a piano pupil of Oscar Peterson and a member of the small ensemble class of John (Dizzy) Gillespie. With Mr. Peterson . . . during a discussion of jazz phrasing, I played some sample four-bar phrases, and waited for the master's reaction. "You know," he said, his voice suddenly in dull, expressionless monotone, "It sure makes a difference how and where you put emphasis on words in a sentence." I nodded. Then he repeated the same sentence, this time in a natural speaking tone with inflections, the words "how" and "where" being most strongly asserted. Now I was getting the point. Next he turned to the keyboard, taking the very phrases I had played, and performing each one twice, speaking, as it were, first in a monotone and then with expressive emphasis. . . . And Mr. Gillespie's class was no less demanding or fruitful. . . . Our instructor was never one to be hesitant about making a point. Once, in the middle of a chorus of "Indiana" in F, Mr. Gillespie suddenly stopped playing and gave me a piercing look. "NEVER play that chord!" he said. Then he parked his incredible horn and took a seat at the piano. What followed was an amazingly lucid 15-minute lecture-demonstration on the use of diminished chords, altered and unaltered. Originally, he had intended to show the virtue of using an E-flat augmented 11th chord in bar 24, but his remarks lengthened into an enlightening discourse on harmonic theory, with many illustrative examples (quite a pianist, Dizzy Gillespie!).[12]

Other student reviews were also extremely positive. One wrote: "It has been the most unique and inspiring single event in my life." Another: "The whole teacher-student experience has been a wonderful experience." And a third directly addressed lecturer Marshall Stearns: "The atmosphere of the school was wonderful. I'd just like to say to you, Mr. Stearns: congratulations, as your course was wonderful." One of the students also reported, "Everyone came to look forward to [the] appearance of Stephanie Barber to see [the] latest costume in her exotic wardrobe." (June Heath recalls that Stephanie had "such grace. She used to walk around in a leotard and a jerkin, like King Arthur.")[13] The students for 1957 who later became jazz musicians were pianist, faculty member at the New England Conservatory, and 1988 MacArthur Fellow Ran Blake; Dave Blume, pianist, vibraphonist, and big band leader; singer, pianist, and composer Bob Dorough; Brazilian bassist Jose de Mello, who also became a jazz critic in Sao Paulo and was the organizer of the first bossa nova festivals; pianist and big band leader John Harmon, who went on to co-found the group Matrix; Dale Hillary, Canadian alto saxophonist; trumpeter John Mason, who played in the Stan Kenton Orchestra; Kent McGarity, trombonist, who played with the Woody Herman band; Dexter Morrill, professor of music at Colgate University; George Moyer, who later studied at the Berklee School of Music in Boston; Tupper Saussy, composer, pianist, and writer, who recorded one jazz album and several rock albums, won three Grammy nominations, and is the author of *The Miracle on Main Street* and *Rulers Of Evil*;[14] Francis Thorne,

The Modern Jazz Quartet and Guests: Third Stream Music (*Atlantic 1345*), *recorded at Music Inn, 1957.*

pianist, who was a composer and recorded one album; and Ian Underwood, alto saxophonist, who made a career as a woodwind and keyboard player, and recorded on many albums (including several with Frank Zappa's Mothers of Invention).[15]

One recording that came out of the 1957 School of Jazz season was *The Modern Jazz Quartet and Guests: Third Stream Music* (Atlantic 1345), which continued the collaboration from a year earlier of the MJQ with Jimmy Giuffre. Two tracks recorded consecutively were Lewis's "Da Capo" and Giuffre's "Fine." Also playing on these tracks were guitarist Jim Hall and bassist Ralph Peña, who together with Giuffre made up the first incarnation of the Jimmy Giuffre 3. The recording of these tracks was actually done at the Music Inn itself on August 24, 1957. Other tracks were recorded later in the studio, using the Beaux Arts String Quartet (Lewis's "Sketch" and Schuller's "Conversation") and a small chamber group of flute, clarinet, French horn, bassoon, cello, and harp (Lewis's "Exposure").[16] The album is now available on CD (Wounded Bird Records WOU 1345).

Before leaving 1957 we should take quick note of the remarkable series of jazz concerts that took place at the Music Barn in the weeks before the School of Jazz was in session. The list reads like a Who's Who of Fifties jazz stars. Appearing from the end of June until mid August were Ella Fitzgerald, Billie Holiday, Ethel Waters, Dave Brubeck, Gerry Mulligan, Lionel Hampton, Duke Ellington, Woody Herman, the Modern Jazz Quartet, and the Jimmy Giuffre trio. Emblematic of the rising prestige of the Music Barn was a change from Baldwin to Steinway for the "official piano" of the concert series. And rounding out the innovations for 1957 was "the Berkshire's [sic] newest gourmet's [sic] attraction," The Potting Shed, a cocktail lounge/restaurant on the grounds of Music Inn, sporting a 56-foot-long bar and serving broiled chicken and steak, beef Stroganoff, and turkey Divan for dinner.[17] Filet mignon "broiled to your preference, served with tossed green salad and potatoes" was $2.95. Also available were lighter snacks as well as "your favorite stingers, tonics, rickeys and brews" (80 cents to $1.10). For the "supper menu" "do-it-yourself" sandwiches as well as other sandwiches and "beef muffins" were served at 80 and 85 cents. Half bottles of Beaujolais and Bordeaux were available for $2.50.[18] The building for the Potting Shed was a former greenhouse on the original estate and was converted to seat about 60 people. An outdoor terrace accommodated another 60.

Dinner menu for the Potting Shed.

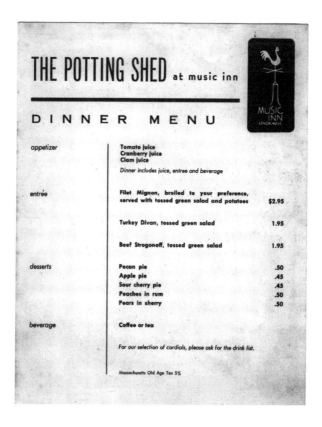

The School of Jazz brought even more publicity to the events at the Barbers' estate. Now mainstream magazines such as the *Saturday Review, Mademoiselle, Charm,* and *Ebony,* as well as the specialist magazines like *Down Beat, Musical Courier, Musical Leader, High Fidelity,* and *Jazz Today* took note of what was going on in Lenox. The almost exclusively classical-music paper, the *Saturday Review,* featured an article by Nat Hentoff on the school, in which he declared that this "new venture . . . marks a pivotal point in the history of jazz."[19] The lengthy article in *Down Beat* reviewed the summer's session and reported that the students "were all fired with the knowledge that they were the pilot class in what well could be one of the most significant advances in jazz."[20] The *New York Times* published several articles on the school, *The Nation* announced its formation, and *Harper's* magazine ran a feature article that drew attention to the seriousness of the enterprise. The article ended with a note that the Newport Jazz Festival had offered $1,000 scholarship money for students for the 1958 session of the Music School. (Tuition in 1957 for three weeks of school as well as room and board was $350.)[21] Newspapers and magazines carried the call for scholarships. In an article in *Metronome,* Nat Hentoff appealed strongly for support for the school from record companies, specifically inviting the owner of Savoy Records, Herman Lubinsky, to contribute. He also pointed out how rare the School of Jazz was. "It will be at least a generation yet before Juilliard and Curtis and Eastman [conservatories] have the sense and sensitivity to our culture to install men like [Max] Roach and [Oscar] Peterson as full faculty members."[22] The article appeared at the end of November 1957. On December 12, the New York *Herald Tribune* announced that the School of Jazz had received a full scholarship grant from Herman Lubinsky "for a promising instrumental student" at the school's next session.

Chapter 9

Purchase of the Wheatleigh Mansion and Flourishing of the School

At the end of 1957, the Barbers bought the Wheatleigh mansion itself – the principal anchor of the estate – from the Boston Symphony Orchestra, which had been using it since 1949 as a dormitory for their Tanglewood students. With it came an additional twenty-five acres of land. They now owned almost all of the Count and Countess's original estate, with the exception of some portions that had been turned into housing lots, a lakefront site that housed the summer camp Camp Mahkeenac (still in operation), and the three original gatehouses that were converted into private homes. In the local newspaper Philip Barber said that the success of the Inn and the School of Jazz obliged them to obtain more space. The mansion would hold an additional fifty guests.[1] In a newsletter to their clients, the Barbers wrote, "Now, luxury lovers who want not only relaxation and space and privacy and good food can also have noble bedrooms with vast private baths, private fireplaces, and some private terraces." By now the Barbers' property comprised 125 acres, and the Inn could accommodate 150 guests.

In February of 1958 the dean of the School, Jules Foster, appeared at a forum of the National Guild of Community Music Schools at the Berkshire Museum to debate the question "What is a Liberal Education in Music?" Proposing the inclusion of jazz in music education were Foster, jazz critic Martin Williams, and jazz piano instructor at Juilliard, John Mehegan; opposing was the gadfly musicologist, author, and composer Nicolas Slonimsky. Foster argued that jazz "has restored the vitality and life to music for the individual" and that jazz was more individualistic and expressionist than classical music. Slonimsky denigrated jazz and said "I don't see that the teaching of jazz is apt to improve our students at all in opposition to what can be learned from the adequate study of more established and certainly more complete music."[2]

In May *Life* listed the Music Barn and the School of Jazz together with Tanglewood as one of the "90 Places of Interest" in the United States.[3] Similar listings appeared in the *New York Times* and the *New Yorker* as well as in a vacation booklet published by the Massachusetts Department of Commerce. In June the *Boston Sunday Herald* reported that the Barbers were also converting a five-story water tower on the property into the central office for the Inn.[4] The tower was known as the "Poodle Tower," since at its base, in a small graveyard marked by stones, were buried the 21 poodles that the Countess de Heredia had owned during her lifetime. Each gravestone was engraved with the dog's name and its birth and death date. The oldest dated back to 1903, the most recent to 1946, the year the Countess died. The water tower had supplied the fountains on the estate with water under pressure and now held the office and a small store. The *Berkshire Eagle* carried a full-length article on Stephanie Barber's "fashion philosophy."[5]

The previous year the Barbers had added The After-Dinner Opera Company to their offerings at the Music Barn. The company was miniature, with three singers and a pianist, and props that could fit into two suitcases. The opera scheduled for 1958 was Leonard Bernstein's *Trouble in Tahiti*, but for some reason the performance was cancelled and a concert by composer and pianist Mary Lou Williams with pianist Pete Johnson was scheduled instead.

The striking success of the Barbers' "little establishment" prompted many newspaper reports from across the country, including articles from the original home of America's jazz, New Orleans, and articles in the black press, such as *Ebony* and the Baltimore *Afro-American*.[6] A story about the School of Jazz appeared in the Finnish journal *Rytmi* for 1958, and *The Metronome Yearbook* for 1958 nominated Philip Barber for a special award "for presenting jazz in delightful surroundings and with a maximum of careful presentations, but, mostly, for his financial backing of the Jazz School, which holds its three-week intensive course on the grounds of Music Inn." The local Berkshire newspaper showed photographs of the inside of the Barbers' home and of the Barbers with their son Chip.[7] The article told the story of the development of the Music Inn, the Music Barn, and the School of Jazz. Philip Barber was reported as spending far more time in Lenox than in New York, as he had moved from president of his company to chairman, which required his presence in New York only two days a week. He was working on a novel. Asked about further expansion of the property, he replied, "This is all we want. Everything is just right for us." At the end of the article, however, the reporter noted that plans were in the works for "a handsome swimming pool."[8]

A letter sent by Stephanie Barber to local businesses to solicit advertisements for the Music Barn program book reprinted many quotes from articles about the Music Inn and the Music Barn for

1958. John Wilson of the *New York Times*: "It's a long trip from dingy backroom dives in New Orleans to a sun-bathed, verdant hillside in the Berkshire Mountains, but jazz has made the journey. . . . The place where this is happening is the Music Barn . . . just down the road a piece from Tanglewood." Leonard Feather of *Downbeat*: "What makes the Music Barn . . . the only place of its kind in the world, is not the music per se. It is the opportunity it provides for musicians, critics, and fans all to meet on a social level." Nat Hentoff, *Downbeat*: "Just one week at Music Inn and the Music Barn is all the more remarkable when viewed against the entire summer season there." And from the *Berkshire Eagle*: "The Music Barn ranks as one of the top jazz centers in the world."

The School of Jazz was also flourishing. The faculty for the summer of 1958 were as follows: Bob Brookmeyer, trombone; Kenny Dorham, trumpet, Jimmy Giuffre, clarinet and saxophone; Jim Hall, guitar; Percy Heath, bass; Milt Jackson, vibraphone; Lee Konitz, saxophone; Max Roach, drums; George Russell, composition; Bill Russo, composition and large ensemble; Marshall Stearns, history of jazz. Individual musicians in residence were Connie Kay, drums; George Coleman, tenor saxophone; Art Davis, bass; Ray Draper, tuba; and Booker Little, trumpet. Professional groups in residence were the Modern Jazz Quartet, the Jimmy Giuffre 3, and the Max Roach Quintet.[9] The 33 students came from 11 states as well as Canada, Holland, Brazil, and Turkey. Fourteen were high-school age, seventeen were in college, and three were in or beyond graduate school. Scholarships were provided by the Newport Jazz Festival, Broadcast Music Incorporated (BMI), Herman Lubinsky, and the School of Jazz Benefit Fund. Courses were offered in Composition and Arranging, the History of Jazz, Large Ensemble, and Small Ensembles, and students also took private lessons. Evening lectures were given on the relationship of jazz to classical music

(Gunther Schuller), teaching opportunities (Herb Pomeroy), jazz festivals (George Wein, Stephanie Barber, and others), jazz recording techniques (Nesuhi Ertegun), and jazz criticism (Martin Williams, Nat Hentoff, and others).

The syllabus for Marshall Stearns's History of Jazz course comprised fifteen lectures, ranging from "Definitions" to "The Future of Jazz" and including listening assignments from the Folkways jazz series,[10] Riverside's *History of Classic Jazz*,[11] Bernstein's *What is Jazz?*,[12] Capitol's *The History of Jazz*,[13] and Langston Hughes's *The Story of Jazz*,[14] and reading assignments from Stearns's own *The Story of Jazz*, Ralph de Toledano's *Frontiers of Jazz*,[15] Sidney Finkelstein's *Jazz: A People's Music*,[16] Winthrop Sargeant's *Jazz Hot and Hybrid*,[17] and Leonard Feather's *Book of Jazz*.[18]

The final concert of the season with faculty and students was held on August 30 as a benefit for the school. It too was well received. In a speech at the concert Philip Barber said that the School of Jazz "represented a democracy of human beings and an aristocracy of talent."[19] The concert included five student combos under the direction of Bob Brookmeyer, Lee Konitz, Max Roach, Jimmy Giuffre, and Kenny Dorham respectively, a large ensemble incorporating the entire student body under the direction of Bill Russo, and a faculty ensemble with a piece by Arif Mardin entitled "Faculty Meeting."

Kenny Dorham spoke later about the great opportunity offered to students by the Lenox School of Jazz:

> When I came to New York as a young boy to play, those fellows wouldn't tell me anything – even Bird, with whom I worked for over a year. If I had this kind of chance *then*, I'd have been poundin' at the gates to get in. I hope these kids realize what they're getting. [20]

One of the things they were getting was a lot of work. The daily schedule ran as follows:

DAILY SCHEDULE OF THE SCHOOL OF JAZZ
1958

Sunday, August 10 – Monday, September 1.

9:00-10:45 a.m.
Composition and Arranging

11:00 a.m. - 12:00 p.m.
History of Jazz, alternate days beginning Tuesday. Jazz Styles and Idioms, alternate days beginning Wednesday.

12:00 p.m. - 2:00 p.m.
Lunch and Free Time (practice, individual lessons.)

2:00 - 5:00 p.m.
Ensemble Rehearsal (Large and small ensembles meet alternate days...schedule to be arranged.)

Private lessons in instruments and composition are arranged individually by student with instructor.

8:30 p.m.
Lectures, panel discussions, or demonstrations by outstanding authorities in the many aspects of the jazz field, including recording, management, criticism, and the relationship between jazz and other fields.

Concerts at the Music Barn that summer included "regulars" Dave Brubeck, Duke Ellington, Lionel Hampton, Wilbur de Paris, Bobby Hackett, Mary Lou Williams, Oscar Peterson, and the Modern Jazz Quartet, with newcomers Anita O'Day and Chris Connor, singers; pianists George Shearing and Joe Turner; and tenor saxophonist Sonny Rollins, who had previously only appeared on a panel discussion but this year played with the Modern Jazz Quartet for the final professional concert of the season. (A recording of this concert was released the following June on the Atlantic label.) The Tony Scott Quintet gave an afternoon of jazz with poetry, featuring readings by Langston Hughes. And on August 17 Max Roach appeared as soloist with the percussion section from the Boston Symphony Orchestra led by percussionist, composer, and conductor Harold Farberman. One of the pieces on that program was Farberman's own *Music Inn Suite*, and a recording of the concert was released in 1959 on Mercury Records.[21] The movements of the suite reflected life at the Inn: "Music Inn," "Poodle Tower," "Soliloquy I," "Potting Shed Passacaglia," "Soliloquy II," "Stephanie B.," "Duo Concertante," "Music Inn." The soliloquies were representations of the reactions of guests to the Inn, one female and one male, and the "Duo Concertante" a conversation between them. Farberman said that "Stephanie B." was "a portrait of the First Lady of Music Inn. One has to meet Stephanie Barber to appreciate her. It can only be said that she is personality, color, and vibrancy personified."[22]

Two other recordings involving faculty members of the School of Jazz were made that summer of 1958. On August 31 the Modern Jazz Quartet concert was recorded including, on two pieces, tenor saxophonist Sonny Rollins. It was released the following June on Atlantic Records (Atlantic 1299).[23] Entitled *The Modern Jazz Quartet at Music Inn, Guest Artist: Sonny Rollins*, it was produced by Nesuhi Ertegun, contained liner notes by Gunther Schuller, and sported an atmospheric photograph of the Music Barn on the front cover.[24] The record has been re-released on CD (Mobile Fidelity 632 and Collectables Jazz Classics COL 7785) and opens with the quartet playing several standards: "Stardust," "I Can't Get Started," "Lover Man," and "Yardbird Suite." There follow two Lewis originals, "Midsummer" and "Festival Sketches." Rollins joins the quartet for the last two tracks, the much harder-swinging "Bags' Groove" and "Night in Tunisia."

The next day, on September 1, just after the close of the school, Jimmy Giuffre began another recording project at Lenox. The result (only partly recorded at Lenox) was *The Four Brothers Sound* (Atlantic 1295), which included Giuffre and two other faculty members: the trombonist Bob Brookmeyer playing piano and guitarist Jim Hall. (This trio became the new Jimmy Giuffre 3.) The title of the album refers to a famous earlier work of Giuffre's – "Four Brothers" – that he had written and arranged for the Woody Herman orchestra in 1947. The saxophonists of the second Herman orchestra (the "Second Herd"), which was formed towards the end of

The Modern Jazz Quartet at Music Inn, Guest Artist: Sonny Rollins (*Atlantic 1299), recorded at Music Inn, 1958.*

1947, gave the band its characteristic sound. They became known as the "Four Brothers."[25] On Giuffre's *The Four Brothers Sound*, the four saxophones are all played by Giuffre in a multi-tracked experiment unusual for 1958. Giuffre said in the liner notes that with multi-tracking "one can get a unique musical sound. . . I wanted a unity of tone and phrasing. . . . I wanted the listener to bathe in the sound." The album contains four Giuffre originals: "Four Brothers," "Ode to Switzerland," "Space," and Giuffre's tribute to the Music Barn, "Blues in the Barn." Giuffre described the Barn as "a wonderful place to play . . . all elements seem to come together there to inspire." On the second side are five standards: "I Gotta Right to Sing the Blues," "Come Rain or Come Shine," "Memphis in June," "Cabin in the Sky," and "Ol' Folks," all of which are given a special sound by the blending of the four tenor saxophones. The liner notes report that the recording session went smoothly apart from some interruptions "in the form of shouted goodbyes from departing students" and "a few happy crickets chirping outside of Music Barn." While the former were edited out, an attentive listener can still hear those happy crickets from the late summer of 1958. (A CD reissue of this album together with *Portrait of the Artist: Bob Brookmeyer* [originally Atlantic 1320, 1960] is available on Collectables Jazz Classics COL 6284.)[26]

Students from the 1958 session of the School of Jazz who went on to careers in jazz included pianists Albert Malacara and Jon Mayer, bassist George Moyer, tenor saxophonist Don Stewart, saxophonist Sture Swenson, who played baritone and bass saxophone with the Stan Kenton band, drummer Bernard Wilkinson, and composer and arranger Arif Mardin, who later won a Grammy award and became Senior Vice-President of Atlantic Records.

The Lenox School of Jazz was starting to be featured more and more in the mainstream press as well as the important trade magazines. In September of 1958, the School was written up in *Newsweek* magazine. Under the heading "Jazz without Juleps," the article drew attention to the seriousness and rigor of the enterprise (as well as its no-alcohol policy). John Lewis gave the rationale for the existence of the school: "The kids of today can't jam informally with the pros as they did years ago. The pros are too busy earning a living, and the music has become too complex. You can't pick it up by osmosis. It must be studied." The studying aspect was reinforced by the accompanying photograph, which depicts three serious young men playing saxophones and is captioned "Cram Session at Lenox."[27]

In October the School printed a one-page newsletter, headed by an appeal from John Lewis for gifts and grants. Lewis wrote that the School had posted a deficit from its first two years of $1,700, despite the fact that all the members of the faculty were working "for living expenses or less."[28] He also pointed out this figure did not include the costs to the Inn, which provided housing and meals for the School at below cost.

Metronome carried two lengthy articles on the School of Jazz in its October and November issues.[29] The tone was highly laudatory. "For every one involved there should be immense applause for one of the most vital movements within jazz, one which will have immeasurable rewards." "[T]here is really no equal today [to the School] . . . for which . . . we have nearly unqualified praise, including in that praise special words for the faculty, the participating musicians, dean Jules Foster, director John Lewis, and the Phil Barbers [sic], who own the property and contribute much to the excellence of the undertaking." *Down Beat* also carried a long article on the school, declaring "What was an exciting possibility a few years ago has become an established reality."[30]

SCHOOL OF jazz

Vol.1 No.1

Oct. 1958

Lenox, Mass.!

DIRECTOR JOHN LEWIS ASKS MUSICAL CHAIRS NEXT YEAR

"WE NEED ENDOWMENT GIFTS for chairs of instruction, to use a University term," declared John Lewin in his report to the Trustees of the School of Jazz.

"Endowed chairs should be set up for drums, piano, sax, trumpet, trombone, & the other instruments; also composition and History of Jazz. These chairs could bear the names of the donors or of distinguished musicians.

"The yearly cost of a chair would be $500.00, to cover salary, board and room of the faculty member and a share of the administrative and teaching costs for the three-week period.

"INSTRUMENT COMPANIES, RECORD COMPANIES and other donors should find this tax-free gift attractive.

"GRANTS TO COVER 2 YEARS are essential. Thus a $1000. grant would provide for a named chair in any subject. These grants would allow us to reduce tuition costs to all, in addition to continuing scholarship grants where necessary.

"THE DEFICIT OF OUR TWO beginning years is $1700. This does not count the additional loan to Music Inn, which has been paid by the School considerably less than its actual costs.

"WE PROVIDE ONE TEACHER for every 3 students for intensive instruction. At going commercial rates the salaries for faculty would be over $40,000, but they are working for living expenses or less because they believe in the School."

FACULTY MEMBERS IN THE FIRST TWO YEARS INCLUDED Bobbie Brookmeyer, Ray Brown, Kenny Dorham, Herb Ellis, Dizzy Gillespie, Jimmy Giuffre, Jim Hall, Percy Heath, Milt Jackson, Lee Konitz, Oscar Peterson, Max Roach, George Russell, Bill Russo, and Marshall Stearns.

ATLANTIC ROYALTY TO SCHOOL OF JAZZ

Release this winter of an LP based on a Voice of America concert at Music Inn with % of royalties to the School of Jazz was told to Trustees by V. P. Neauhi Ertegun. See next bulletin for name and release date.

INFORMATION, MAN!
We want news about faculty and alumni for publication in the next bulletin.

PLEASE SEND FACTS OF YOUR JAZZ LIFE to Dean Jule Foster, School of Jazz, Lenox, Massachusetts.

SCHOLARSHIPS REPORT

NEWPORT's Louis Armstrong awards went to guitarist Robert Cairns, Edmonton, Canada; 2nd yr. trumpet man John Mason, Chicago, Ill; Jon Mayer, piano, N.Y.C.; Don Stewart, tenor, of Bloomington, Ind.; & Dom Turkowski, baritone, Boston.

B.M.I.'s grant went to composer Arif Mardin, of Istanbul, Turkey.

HERMAN LUBINSKY award to 2nd year Dale Hilary of Edmonton, Canada, tenor.

GREAT SOUTH BAY AWARD to clarinetist Robert Gordon, Manhasset, N.Y.

S. of J. Benefit Scholarships to Bradley Jones, trombone, Jamestown, N.Y.; Albert Malacura, piano, Amarillo, Tex; 2nd year Kent McGarity, trombone, Norwich, N.Y.; James Millard, trumpet, Newburgh, N.Y.; Bernard Wilkinson, drums, Brooklyn, N.Y.

ELECTRIC BODY TYPE COURTESY OF BROADCAST MUSIC, INC.

COMPOSERS PLAN FOR RECORD DATE

Bill Russo, George Russell, Jimmy Giuffre and John Lewin are now at work on compositions for a School of Jazz LP. Deadline which the men have set for themselves is Thanksgiving. The record date, played by the allstar faculty, will be set as soon as bookings allow.

Noted camera man Clem Kalisher has offered cover photo and critic Martin Williams will do liner notes. Atlantic will record and entire profit of the LP will go to cutting down tuition costs of the non-profit School of Jazz at Lenox.

BOARD OF TRUSTEES FOR '59 ANNOUNCED

Newsletter from the School of Jazz, October, 1958.

Chapter 10

The 1959 Season: Apogee
of the School,
Arrival of "Student" Ornette Coleman,
Problems of Success

It was in the year 1959 that the School of Jazz reached its apogee, while in that same year certain events began to foreshadow the change in the atmosphere of the times that would soon lead to the School's demise. In January of 1959, *Esquire* magazine published a jazz issue, dedicated to "The Golden Age of Jazz" and containing Art Kane's famous "Great Day in Harlem" photograph featuring dozens of the great contemporary musicians in jazz. In an article on the current jazz scene, "The Golden Age: Time Present," John Clellon Holmes mentions Lenox, Massachusetts, as the place where clarinetists Jimmy Giuffre and Pee Wee Russell "stood side by side . . . and traded choruses with one another on the blues, which is the foundation of both their styles, no matter how utterly unlike they may sound."[1] Holmes (1926-1988) was a poet, essayist, and novelist, who wrote about the Beat generation in a novel of 1952 (*Go*)[2] and in an important piece entitled "This Is the Beat Generation" in the *New York Times* magazine for the same year.[3]

Cue magazine's *Annual Register of Distinctive Dining in City and Country* for 1959 listed the Music Inn as one of "the most pleasurable," "superb" resorts on the East Coast.[4] *Metronome's* Year Book, *An Introduction to Jazz 1959*, carried several photographs from past sessions in Lenox, including a jam session with Connie Kay, Max Roach, Oscar Pettiford, Dick Katz, Herbie Mann, Teo Macero, Teddy Charles and others; Gigi Gryce trying out a bow and arrow; and a delighted Gerry Mulligan watching a dance rehearsal. *Saturday Review* reviewed some recent jazz recordings, including the *Historic Jazz Concert* recording of 1956, only recently released, and, with reference to Richard Wagner's custom-built opera house in southern Germany, described the Music Inn as a "clapboard jazz Bayreuth." [5] And the Music Barn was recommended to readers in the pages of *Playboy* magazine in May of 1959.[6]

In addition to the Modern Jazz Quartet, another famous quartet was in residence at the School of Jazz that summer. This was the Dave Brubeck Quartet, which had become one of the most popular and successful small jazz groups in the world. The Quartet had won the *Playboy* readers' poll three years in a row, and in 1959 the Quartet won *Down Beat* magazine's readers' poll. Brubeck also had one of the few integrated combos in jazz at that time, and he was a principled fighter against discrimination. The following season Brubeck would cancel a month-long tour of colleges in the South (and forfeit over $40,000) because many of these enlightened centers of learning objected to his racially integrated band. He also refused to appear on television shows which were determined not to show his black bass player, Eugene Wright, on camera.

In February of 1959, a grant of six scholarships to the School was made by the Schaefer brewing company.[7] Another new scholarship was given by the Great South Bay Jazz Festival of New York,

Telegram to Stephanie Barber explaining the cancellation of Louis Armstrong's appearance at the Music Barn, June, 1959.

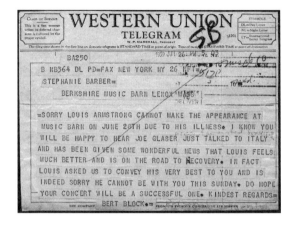

while the grants from the Newport Jazz Festival and Savoy Records continued. BMI increased its grant from $385 to $1,000 and gave the money in the name of John Lewis.[8] Joe Glaser (Louis Armstrong's manager), Atlantic Records, United Artists, and Norman Granz all gave money; and a scholarship was provided in memory of Harvey Huston, a jazz disc jockey. For 1959 scholarship funds reached almost $10,000.[9] An appeal for more was made by jazz journalist Ralph Gleason in his column in the *San Francisco Chronicle*. Referring to the deficit at the school, he called for more musicians and record companies to contribute, for "[t]here are few projects that enjoy the stature within the field that the School of Jazz does."[10] An article in *Coronet* drew attention to women's contributions to the business of jazz, citing, among others, "Stephanie Barber, who has made Music Inn at Lenox, Massachusetts, so successful."[11] That spring the School held auditions in New York for students from Boston University, Colgate, Cornell, Harvard, Holy Cross, Lehigh, the University of Pennsylvania, Princeton, Rutgers, Union, and Yale. Other students could apply by sending a tape and filling out a short musical exam. Seven students won scholarships.[12] In all forty-five students attended the 1959 session of the school, hailing from fifteen states and four foreign countries, one as far away as India.

The Music Barn series was to open with Louis Armstrong again and had an extraordinary number of the greatest names in jazz on the roster. In addition to those who had played at the Barn before, such as Armstrong, Basie, Brubeck, Giuffre, the MJQ, Kenton, Seeger, Shearing, Rollins and Vaughan, newcomers scheduled were Miles Davis with his quintet, the young jazz pianist Ahmad Jamal, the Kingston Trio – a folk group that had made a spectacular success with their recent recording of "Tom Dooley" – the Lambert, Hendricks, and Ross vocal trio, the Dukes of Dixieland, and soul singer Ray Charles. Five days before the opening of the season, on June 23rd, Louis Armstrong suffered a heart attack in Spoleto, Italy, and had to cancel his concert in Lenox.[13] His doctor, worried about damaging publicity, insisted that Armstrong had pneumonia. The *Berkshire Eagle* managed to come up with the dramatic, if irresponsible, headline: "Armstrong Is Gravely Ill, Now in Coma."[14] Fortunately the jazz legend, by then in his late fifties, recovered very quickly. A telegram to Stephanie Barber from Bert Block (who was a band leader and booking agent),[15] dated June 26, read as follows:

SORRY LOUIS ARMSTRONG CANNOT MAKE THE APPEARANCE AT MUSIC BARN ON JUNE 28TH DUE TO HIS ILLNESS. I KNOW YOU WILL BE HAPPY TO HEAR JOE GLASER [Armstrong's manager] JUST TALKED TO ITALY AND HAS BEEN GIVEN SOME WONDERFUL NEWS THAT LOUIS FEELS MUCH BETTER AND IS ON THE ROAD TO RECOVERY. IN FACT LOUIS ASKED US TO CONVEY HIS VERY BEST TO YOU AND IS INDEED SORRY HE CANNOT BE WITH YOU THIS SUNDAY. DO HOPE YOUR CONCERT WILL BE A SUCCESSFUL ONE.

Wilbur de Paris and his New Orleans Jazz Band opened the season instead. Trombonist de Paris was no slouch in the music world. He had been playing since the early Twenties, knew Armstrong from their New Orleans days, and had played in the Ellington orchestra for several years in the Forties. Two years earlier he and his band had been chosen by the State Department to tour Africa. A review of the last-minute concert praised the "pure jubilation in the 'stompers' and smooth wailing in the blues, all backed by sound arrangements and [the] display of individual skill" and singled out the lead trumpeter Doc Cheatham as "especially outstanding."[16]

Many concerts from that banner year received rave reviews. In a review of July 8 in the *Berkshire Eagle*, the Basie band was hailed as "[t]he best big band in the business."

> [T]he Count Basie Orchestra rocked an audience of 800 at the Music Barn in Lenox last night with a sound that defied description. . . . It was a multi-colored, multi-varied, beautiful, clean torrent of melody and rhythm that blended in a harmonic pattern of feeling and emotion. By their playing this band defines the term "swing" to an exact degree.[17]

At the George Shearing Quintet concert, "[the pianist] and the audience had a ball. Shearing has the heart-warming capacity to make his listeners have as much pure *fun* as he does in performing."[18] The Stan Kenton Orchestra "competed with a noisy, drenching rain at the Music Barn in Lenox Sunday evening and drowned out the competition."[19] "The music had vibrancy and color, a kaleidoscope quality . . ."[20] For the Dave Brubeck Quartet "the largest crowd of the season was treated to some outstanding improvisation and a few tempos [sic] that haven't been heard in this area since Moondog graced the same stage in the dim dead days of

1955."[21] The writer is presumably referring to the unusual *meters* of some of the items, since the group played four pieces from their forthcoming *Time Out* album, including Desmond's catchy "Take Five." Sarah Vaughan showed off her "fabulous technique" in over twenty songs, and, after one encore, "had to beg off before the crowd would let her be."[22] The crowd at Ahmad Jamal's concert was "in orbit."[23] And an overall assessment of the Music Barn offerings concluded that "The Barbers can't seem to miss with their Music Barn located in the 'backyard' of Tanglewood, for no matter what they present, the place is filled to capacity."[24]

The popularity of the events at the Barn became a problem at the end of July. The Kingston Trio, whose "Tom Dooley" and "M.T.A." (about the man who got lost on the Boston subway) were nationwide hits, attracted a crowd of nearly three thousand people. Gatecrashers crawled over the roof of the barn and ripped out the wires to the loudspeakers that were intended to broadcast the music to the overflow crowd on the lawn. Alcohol was brought illegally onto the premises, members of the audience became rowdy, a young female usher was hit in the face, and people attempted to gain access to the concert through fire doors and other access points. One group of would-be ticket buyers actually tried to lift the twenty-by-twenty-foot wooden ticket office off its foundations. Finally the State Police had to be called. The fracas produced recriminations in the newspapers and elicited a public apology by the Barbers.[25] It was an unfortunate premonition of events that would force the closing of the Music Inn twenty years later.

Unfortunately a second incident marred the reputation of the jazz venue soon after the first. Miles Davis, who was due to play on August 9 at the Music Barn after returning from a tour of the West coast and Midwest, suddenly canceled at the last minute. (This was a week before the scheduled release of his seminal album *Kind of Blue*.) A scramble put together some performances by students and faculty of the School of Jazz, who had only just started arriving for the start of school that very day. The concert was lambasted in the papers as "desperately dull," and the Music Barn was criticized, with typical journalistic zeal, as being the focus of "several" "justified" complaints over the summer.[26] Stephanie, however, reported that Davis "got here at midnight after the audience had waited for [three] hours. We gave back everybody's money. He never said, 'I'm sorry.' He played for all the kids, the staff, and whoever was around in the fields. He went out into the fields and gave them a 2 a.m. concert. He was the only person we ever sued because he broke his contract. I was surprised, but John Lewis was with Phil on that. He was furious."[27]

Refunds had to be handed out to over three hundred people when the tour bus carrying Ray Charles and his group broke down on the way to a concert scheduled for August 23. The performers arrived at 9:45 p.m., "but by that time the patrons were gone and the Barn was dark." Engineers from Atlantic Records were also disappointed. They had spent two days setting up equipment to tape the concert.[28] (Members of the band did organize a jam session with the students later that night.) The *Lakeville Journal*, which had exaggerated the number of complaints about the Music Barn two weeks earlier, blamed the Barbers for this mishap also: "The management offered no explanation other than the fact that the guest artists 'didn't show.'"[29]

But the encomiums for the jazz concerts continued. The early-August concert by the Modern Jazz Quartet produced "real swinging, solid, exciting jazz of the finest kind."[30] The performance by the Bobby Hackett Quartet was described as "[r]elaxed, easy, humorous, and most pleasant."[31] The Modern Jazz Quartet gave their second concert of the season towards the end of August, when they were joined by student Al Kiger on trumpet for "How High the Moon," faculty guitarist Jim Hall for "Slowly" and "Pyramid," and in a surprise appearance, Dizzy Gillespie for three tunes. The Quartet also premiered some of John Lewis's new work on a film score for *Odds Against Tomorrow* (1959, dir. Robert Wise, starring Harry Belafonte).[32]

A final disappointment accompanied the scheduled concert of Sonny Rollins on September 6 when it was cancelled by the saxophonist only a short time before the event. (Rollins told me that he decided to take a break from performing "to go back and do some more studying. I was always a self-taught musician, and by '59 I had a lot of accolades, and being a person who was always seeking my own counsel I realized that I was deficient in a lot of musical aspects – things that I had not dealt with coming up. I was proud of that [taking time off] – it took a lot of self discipline.")[33] The final concert of the season, therefore, turned out to be the one that had occurred the previous night with the Dukes of Dixieland. The season therefore ended as it had begun, with a cancellation and the quick substitution of a traditional New Orleans band. However the audience was reported to be "delighted" with the music.[34]

As for the School of Jazz, the contrast between its financial health and its musical accomplishments was stark. In July of 1959, a syndicated article by the jazz writer Ralph Gleason drew attention once again to the operating deficit of the school. Appearing in various newspapers around the country, Gleason's article was headlined "First Jazz School Expanding; Financial Woes Mounting, Too" in at least one newspaper[35] and "School of Jazz Has Everything But Cash" in another.[36] However the reputation of the School had never been higher. In the *Herald Tribune* magazine for July 26, 1959, a feature article by Nat Hentoff described the school as "the only school of its kind," where "jazz flourishes more fully than ever before."[37] And the *Boston Herald* called the Lenox School of Jazz "the most unique institution in the individualistic world of jazz."[38]

For the 1959 session, three tents were purchased by the School for use as rehearsal space and practice studios. A portion of the Music Inn dining room was partitioned off to provide another rehearsal space.

Students did not waste time while they were in attendance at the School. Several articles focused on the amount of work the students had to put in during their summers. The *Washington Post* and *Times Herald* profiled a student from Princeton, bassist John Keyser, whose work day included seven hours of lectures and practice, with concerts and lectures in the evenings, and time for only five hours of sleep.[39] The *Hartford Courant* explained that while summer is vacation time for most people, the students at Lenox were spending three weeks doing nothing but "work, work, work."[40] A paragraph about the School in the *Berkshire Eagle* accompanied a photo spread of students rehearsing, practicing, (and falling asleep) late that August. "For three weeks," it said, "they have jazz from breakfast through dinner, hear jazz lectures at night and fall asleep to the strains of late jam sessions."[41]

The *Berkshire Eagle* used the Music Barn and Wheatleigh as the backdrop for a fashion shoot at the end of August. Modeling "transitional" dresses in cotton were Michaela Maguire from the nearby town of Pittsfield and Russell, artist and wife of the jazz composer on the faculty of the School, George Russell, later to become the wife of Jimmy Giuffre. She is resplendent in a "copper-and-black striped transitional, with a wide-collared jacket cover[ing] a strapless sheath top of copper cotton."[42]

Students from the 1959 session of the Lenox School of Jazz who went on to careers in jazz included David Baker, who became a well-known jazz educator, author, theorist, composer, and professor of music; John Bergamo, percussionist and composer; Ran Blake, whose career was summarized earlier (he was a student at Lenox for all four years the School was in existence); Nico Bunink, a Dutch pianist, who performed with Mingus in the early Sixties and continued to perform in Europe throughout his life; Ted Casher, a tenor saxophonist, who performed actively in the Boston area; Don Cherry, trumpeter, who played with Ornette Coleman in the Fifties and early Sixties, became a catalyst in the World Music movement, and went on to make hundreds of recordings; John Eckert, a trumpeter who played in both classical and jazz ensembles as well as for rock groups; Peter Farmer, a trumpet and saxophone player and composer; Herb Gardner, trombonist, teacher, and composer; Barry Greenspan, a drummer, who ran a drum store in New York City; Tony Greenwald, a trumpet player, who played in Herb Pomeroy's big band in Boston and became a professor of psychology; Margo Guryan, composer and songwriter; Al Kiger, a trumpeter who recorded with John Lewis, George Russell, and others; Steve Kuhn, pianist, who played with Kenny Dorham, was a member of the original John Coltrane Quartet, and went on to a prolific career; David Lahm, composer and active pianist; Gary McFarland, vibraphonist, composer, and arranger; David Mackay, a prolific and active pianist; Lenny Popkin, alto saxophonist; Larry Ridley, a bass player, who worked with many of the top names in jazz and taught at Rutgers University; Perry Robinson, clarinetist, who led an extremely active career and appeared on over one hundred recordings;[43] Edward Saldanha, pianist, who recorded and performed in India; Don Stewart, tenor saxophonist; Sture Swenson, whose career was summarized earlier (he was at the School for two years); Ian Underwood (previously a student in 1957); and Attila Zoller, a guitarist from Hungary, who founded the Vermont Jazz Center.[44]

Appearing in a photograph in the New York *Herald Tribune* at

*Ornette Coleman
at the Lenox School
of Jazz, 1959.*

the very end of August (and on the last day of the school) was one more student of that summer: an alto saxophonist who turned out to be the most famous student the School of Jazz ever had: Ornette Coleman, who went on to turn the jazz world upside down with his concept of Free Jazz, won the first-ever Guggenheim Fellowship for jazz composition as well as a $360,000 MacArthur Foundation "genius" award, and was inducted into *Down Beat*'s Hall of Fame.[45] A major analysis of the history of jazz published in 2001 places

Ornette Coleman in the pantheon of the most important jazz innovators of the twentieth century, alongside Armstrong, Parker, Gillespie, Davis, and Coltrane.[46]

Coleman made quite an impression at Lenox in the summer of 1959. And, truth to tell, he was not really a student any more. He had been playing professionally for over ten years, had recorded three albums already, and had founded the quartet, with Don Cherry, Charlie Haden, and Billy Higgins, that would revolutionize jazz. The three albums were: *Something Else!!!!: The Music of Ornette Coleman* (Contemporary COP 024), recorded in February and March of 1958; *Tomorrow Is the Question: The New Music of Ornette Coleman* (Contemporary COP 002), recorded in January, February and March, 1959; and *The Shape of Jazz to Come* (Atlantic 1317), recorded on May 22 of that year. He was twenty-nine years old. Earlier in the year he had caught the attention of John Lewis, who had introduced him to the Atlantic label. Lewis also arranged for Coleman and Don Cherry to attend the School of Jazz on scholarship. He told an interviewer that he found their music "very fresh and interesting."[47] Cherry was twenty-three and was also pictured in a newspaper that year in a feature on the School of Jazz.[48]

Apparently it was the teachers who learned from Coleman that summer. Gunther Schuller wrote that Jimmy Giuffre "was trying to play a kind of Ornette Coleman on tenor" and that Coleman "could have taught any of the faculty at Lenox."[49] Giuffre reported that it was "wonderful . . . when somebody gets to this point where he can be this free and this sure in his statement. . . ."[50] Coleman's playing was not uncontroversial, for trombonist and composer Bob Brookmeyer, an important figure in West Coast jazz, quit the faculty in protest.[51] Members of the faculty were divided over Coleman's new approach. A local newspaper described the situation:

This year there appeared at the school a 29-year-old saxophonist from the West Coast named Ornette Coleman. This talented young man split the faculty of the school smack down the middle because he plays in a style that is uniquely his own, a chaotic effusion that enraged the more traditionally oriented of the teachers. . . . [T]he students were terribly shook [sic]. . . .[T]hey found. . . several sects fighting a battle that had no beginning, middle, or end. It was exciting to be in the middle of it, but they never knew from which direction they might be clobbered.[52]

And Gunther Schuller wrote that "everyone (including the faculty) seemed to be stunned . . . by the impact of Coleman and Cherry."[53]

Ornette Coleman, who is a man of deep humility (and who speaks in a fascinatingly oblique and elliptical manner), remembers it differently. In an interview for his seventy-fifth birthday, when I asked him about his experience at Lenox, he told me that John Lewis and Gunther Schuller "had put together all the people who were interesting."

It was fine, but it had more to do with the teachers . . . who were analyzing what you were doing. They were confused about how to accept what I was doing. . . . None of them was playing like [us]. . . . All of these experiences made me understand that certain people were gifted to do certain things. It made me understand that the quality of music as far as their knowledge was one thing; the expression and the sound was another. So they were very interested in how we were playing.

JY: So in a way some of the teachers were learning from you?

OC: Well, I think they were learning from the overall concept of what all of that means.

JY: From what you and Don were doing?
OC: Yes.[54]

Three of Coleman's compositions from his first two albums were featured on the final concert of the summer put on by faculty and students. This concert was reviewed in the local paper.

> Best individual performances of the evening were turned in by pianist Ran Blake and alto saxophonist Ornette Coleman. Young Blake has tremendous talent both as a composer and a player, and his rendition of his own "Vanguard" had wonderful feeling and expressiveness. . . . The 29-year-old Coleman created quite a stir at the school this season with his unique style and theories, and the short hearing Saturday night was a revelation both as to style and creativity. Three of his originals were played by the small ensemble, and they were quite interesting. This West Coast musician is obviously about to embark on the crucial voyage of his career. . . . [55]

And *Down Beat*, which also reviewed the concert, wrote that Coleman "has a driving, exciting, highly individual style."[56]

More importantly, as a result of hearing Coleman play that summer in Lenox, the well-regarded critic and *Jazz Review* co-editor Martin Williams arranged for the Coleman Quartet to make its first appearance in New York later that year (at the Five Spot Café), an appearance that touched off a firestorm of controversy that has still not completely abated. He also wrote the following deeply-felt and remarkably prescient comments in the *Jazz Review* for October under the heading "A Letter from Lenox, Mass.":

> I honestly believe . . . that what Ornette Coleman is doing on alto will affect the whole character of jazz music profoundly and pervasively. [When he played in Lenox]

> . . . it was as if he opened up something in one's soul and
> opened up the way for jazz to grow. His music makes a
> new sensibility for one's ears and heart and mind, all the
> while including the most fundamental things in jazz. . . .
> The step he is taking, like all great steps, seems inevitable
> only when someone has taken it . . . [57]

The article was accompanied by a full-page photo of Coleman
sitting on a split-rail fence on the property with his saxophone case
at his feet.

Remarkably there is a private recording that captured some of
the performances from that evening on August 29, 1959. It holds
eleven tracks on two sides of a ten-inch LP, one or two tracks from
each of the groups showcased that night. The concert itself presented six groups – led by Gunther Schuller; Bill Evans, Jim Hall,
and Connie Kay; Kenny Dorham; Max Roach and John Lewis;
Jimmy Giuffre; and Herb Pomeroy – playing a total of twenty-six
selections. Coleman played in the Max Roach – John Lewis ensemble, with Don Cherry on trumpet, Kent McGarity on trombone,
Steve Kuhn (for one tune Ron Brown) on piano, Larry Ridley on
bass, and Barry Greenspan on drums. The group played three tunes
of Coleman's – "The Sphinx," "Compassion," and "Giggin'," – and
Margo Guryan's "Inn Tune." The first and the last are preserved on
the private recording.[58] "The Sphinx" comes from Coleman's 1958
album *Something Else!!!: The Music of Ornette Coleman*, his first
commercial recording. It is one of the earliest examples of the kind
of bi-tempo tunes that became Coleman's signature, where a jaunty
mood is tellingly juxtaposed with one that is mournful. ("Compassion" and "Giggin'" are tunes Coleman recorded on *Tomorrow Is the
Question*.) Margo Guryan's "Inn Tune" is relaxed and easy swinging.
On both tracks one can hear clearly the saxophonist's distinctively
confident, fluid, wailing, edgy sound and his totally original ap-

proach to improvisation, which is based not on chord changes but on melodic, motivic, and rhythmic aspects of a tune. The idiosyncrasies of the recording make Don Cherry harder to hear, though he also makes his presence felt.[59] Enthusiastic applause may be heard after one of Coleman's improvised solos.

The concert as a whole was discussed in an article in *Metronome* that October. The author, Jack Maher, wrote: "The number of really first-class musicians was phenomenal; each of the groups had two and sometimes three or four first-class players. But even more imposing was the wonderful unity with which most of the groups played. Their material was well under their hands and their poise and their dynamic sense [were] well under control."[60] That same month *Down Beat* carried an article on the school that was also primarily composed of a review of the final concert. "[I]t was instantly clear," the magazine reported, "that no one had been idle during the weeks of rehearsal and study. . . . [T]he musicianship of the entire student body was of a high caliber."[61]

The literary world gradually came to see Ornette Coleman as an emblematic figure. Thomas Pynchon's novel *V* is set in the mid Fifties, and one of the characters is named McClintic Sphere. (This name is designed to suggest a mixture of Ornette Coleman and Thelonious Monk. Pynchon invents the name McClintic to suggest Scotland, since the name Coleman is Scottish, and Thelonious Monk's second name was Sphere). The book character is a saxophonist from Fort Worth (where Coleman was born), who plays at a New York club called the V-Note (a combination of the Five Spot and the Blue Note). He plays in a pianoless quartet (Coleman's own quartet had no piano), and his sideman was "a boy he had found in the Ozarks who blew a natural horn in F." (Don Cherry was born in Oklahoma City and played a pocket cornet.) His girlfriend's name is Ruby. (One of Monk's best-known tunes is "Ruby, My Dear.") He

Cover of program for the Potting Shed, 1959.

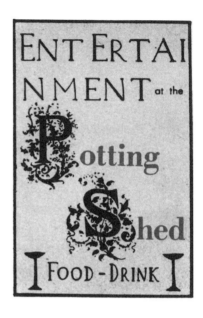

plays an ivory alto (Coleman played a white plastic alto), and his sound "was like nothing any of them had heard before. . . . There were people around, mostly those who wrote for Downbeat magazine or the liners of LP records, who seemed to feel he played disregarding chord changes completely." Finally, McClintic spends part of the summer in Lenox, Massachusetts, at "that jazz festival," and he sends Ruby "postcards showing different views of Tanglewood and the Berkshires once a week."[62]

The jazz festival at Newport was still only a four-day event, whereas the Folk and Jazz Festival at Music Inn lasted for several weeks. In 1959, there were 27 events at the Music Barn, running from the end of June to the beginning of September. The Barbers' Music Inn may have had a stronger influence on Newport than has previously been recognized. Perhaps inspired by both the folk music and the educational aspects of his Music Inn experience in 1956 (remember that pianist who received shouted instructions?), the impresario and founder of the Newport Festival George Wein made two influential changes in 1959. He inaugurated the Newport Folk Festival. And both the jazz festival and the folk festival began to offer educational opportunities. The jazz festival featured "three morning symposiums," and Wein began the Newport Folk Festival that year with a "seminar open to the public."[63]

Encouraged by Newport and perhaps also by the Music Inn, jazz festivals in North America were now quite widespread. The Newport Jazz Festival was still the largest, but there were jazz festivals in the summer of 1959 at Randall's Island, New York, in Boston (put on by Wein in conjunction with Sheraton Hotels), in Toronto, at Purdue University and French Lick in Indiana, and at festivals in Hollywood-by-the-Sea in Florida and Monterey, California. New festivals were started in Detroit and Chicago (the *Playboy* Jazz Festival).[64]

Never content to rest on their laurels, the Barbers introduced yet another musical feature at the Music Inn for 1959. The restaurant and bar on the grounds, the Potting Shed, had been refurbished and now offered live entertainment throughout the season, five evenings a week. Appearing that summer were flamenco guitarist and singer Anita Sheer, jazz singer Mark Murphy, harmonica player Larry Adler, pianist Ellis Larkins, the Dick Katz Quartet, comedian Isobel Robbins, and folk singers Don Poulin, Leon Bibb, and Josh White.[65]

While Marshall Stearns continued his course on the history of jazz, an addition to the curriculum at the School for 1959 was a new course taught by Gunther Schuller entitled "The Analytical History of Jazz." Also new to the teaching staff were Herb Pomeroy (who led a big band of his own and taught at the Berklee School of Music in Boston), taking over the large ensemble teaching, and Bill Evans, who shared the piano teaching with John Lewis. Dave

Brubeck and his wife and five children were staying at the Music Inn from early July to Labor Day. Absent from the faculty that year due to conflicting engagements were Dizzy Gillespie, Oscar Peterson, and Ray Brown.[66] Stephanie later told a charming story about Brubeck's daughter, who was only eight years old that summer. The Brubecks were staying in the Studio, which was part of the Music Barn, and you could hear the music clearly, especially at night during the performances. "She had long blonde braids . . . [and] she came right on stage in the middle of the concert with her hands on her hips and said, 'How do you expect a guy to get any sleep around here?' It broke up the band, the audience, everything. It was very sweet."[67]

The Lenox School for Jazz provided a site for racial mixing that was extremely unusual in the 1950s. Even more unusual was the reversal of roles in which black teachers were teaching white students. As one newspaper wrote, "[I]n the heart of the Berkshires, where Bluebloods and direct descendants of the Mayflower voyagers abound, [there] is this small colony of refugees from Greenwich Village – of all racial types and backgrounds – somehow fused by a common interest in modern music."[68] "At Music Inn, it wasn't about black and white, but blue, as in the blues," says Benjamin Barber. "Jazz helped desegregate America, and as a result helped civilize it."[69] However the students were mostly white. Photographs of the students reveal a sea of white faces, with at most one or two black students per summer. Numbers are impossible to determine, however. Stephanie explained: "Somebody [asked] me from the New York Times, 'How many black students and how many white students do you have?' I said to him, 'I've never counted!'"[70] Benjamin Barber said that for Stephanie "color simply didn't register."[71] In an article in 2004 in the *Berkshire Eagle* for Black History Month, Diane Gordon remembered Stephanie's contributions to racial relations in the Berkshires. She wrote, "Music Inn

Take Five: Mrs. Brubeck takes her five children to the beach, summer 1959.

co-founder Stephanie Barber's relationship with jazz is another example of Berkshire County's patronage of black culture. Gone, but never forgotten, Stephanie Barber's creation of the Lenox School of Jazz is a notable moment in the development of our country's greatest art form."[72]

Women were also a rarity among the students at the school. In the summer of 1959, there were only two women among the forty-five students ("43 men and two girls" as the Brooklyn *Record* put it.)[73] Patronizing attitudes were common. A female bass player was described in the local newspaper as wearing a "black drape and horn-rimmed glasses" and as being "absolutely the cutest bass player I have ever heard pluck a string."[74] The typical attitude of the time was conveyed by an article in *Down Beat* entitled: "Women in Jazz: Do They Belong?"[75]

The Lenox School of Jazz was to have been the first port of call in 1959 for an ambitious documentary film directed by the German jazz scholar Joachim-Ernst Berendt. The crew was scheduled to start filming in Lenox for the last few days of the session and then go on to over a dozen cities across the United States. The film was to have been produced by Sudwestfunk, the Southwest German Radio Network (in what was then called "free" Germany), in conjunction with the U.S. State Department, but was cancelled by the State Department without explanation a few days before the project was to start. Newspapers were critical of the cancellation. The *Oakland Tribune* wrote that "it strengthens the suspicion here at home that the State Department, at heart, still refuses to accept the fact that jazz is our most potent envoy in spreading our message of freedom among foreign peoples. Buttressing the belief are such instances as the government's refusal to book a representation of this musical form at the Brussels World's Fair and [a similar refusal] to insist on its inclusion in the Moscow exhibit."[76]

The State Department may have been wary of figures in the jazz world. In 1957 Armstrong refused to go abroad on a State-Department sponsored tour during the Little Rock, Arkansas, school integration crisis and spoke out forcefully against President Eisenhower's dithering over the affair. As a result Dave Brubeck and his wife Iola (a lyricist) wrote an anti-racism show entitled *The Real Ambassadors*, featuring Louis Armstrong and based on his political stance. It is a satire of the State-Department-sponsored tours for American jazz bands and is overtly political, containing references to the United Nations, American idealism, diplomacy, chaos, and conflict. (A recording was made in 1961, which contains one of Armstrong's most moving performances, the song "They Say I Look Like God.")[77] The Cold War was at its height, and the situation in Berlin was already very tense in 1959, although it was not to become a full-scale crisis until 1961. In the late Fifties about 150,000 people fled from East Germany to the West each year, and Kruschev had imposed a deadline for the withdrawal of the Western powers from the city. The deadline was ultimately withdrawn, the occupying nations agreed to four-way talks, and Kruschev visited the United States in September of 1959. A hiatus in the tension obtained until the Soviets and East Germany escalated the confrontation again in 1961. But Berendt's film was never made.[78]

During the 1959 session, representatives of Voice of America spent a week in Lenox. As a result news concerning the activities of the School was broadcast in several languages across Europe.

The School of Jazz was featured in national magazines again that year. The *Saturday Evening Post* carried a feature story on Mahalia Jackson in which she discussed her appearances at the Music Inn and the School.[79] And *Life* devoted a special issue[80] to "The Good Life," with a section on creativity, featuring poetry, photography, and music workshops around the country, with a captioned photograph from Lenox among others from the Idyllwild Arts Foundation, California (showing Ansel Adams); Bread Loaf Writers' Conference, Vermont (Robert Frost); and Interlochen, Michigan (classical bass player Oscar Zimmerman). The Lenox photo shows a student bending low to study the fingering of MJQ bassist Percy Heath. The introduction to the magazine mirrored the new social realities of the late Fifties by explaining its focus thus: "The new leisure is here. For the first time a civilization has reached a point where most people are no longer preoccupied exclusively with providing food and shelter. The shrinking work week now gives us about 75 free, waking hours as compared with a bare 55 two generations ago."[81] During that winter Stephanie Barber was photographed in the society pages of the local newspaper sporting one of the hats from her spectacular private collection.[82]

The 1960 season marked the tenth anniversary of the founding of
Music Inn and the fourth year of the School of Jazz. The musical
and intellectual content of the Inn's offerings had grown from two
weeks of roundtable discussions and a handful of performances
to a six-week-long festival that showcased some of the top names
in folk and jazz, as well as an established school of jazz that offered a three-week-long session of serious study and performance
for nearly fifty students working with fifteen or sixteen full-time
teachers, performers, coaches, bandleaders and scholars. But 1960
was also destined to be the last year of the School; and even that
season almost didn't happen.

The Inn could now accommodate 150 guests, and the property
encompassed 125 acres, with streams, hills, country walks, tennis
courts, a restaurant, a nightclub, and several kinds of accommoda-

tion ranging from cozy to elegant. Casual music making took place at the Potting Shed and at jam sessions all over the property. The formal concerts at the Music Barn, starting its sixth season, were drawing up to (and sometimes over) 1,000 people. By the time of the 1960 season the Barn had presented over 100 shows. The festival was one of the major jazz venues for touring groups in the country, and the School, which had acquired a nationwide reputation, was featured in both mainstream magazines and specialty journals across the country as well as in Collier's *Encyclopedia Yearbook* for 1960. Festival concerts for 1960 featured Louis Armstrong (making up for his unfortunate cancellation of the year before), Dave Brubeck, George Shearing, Mahalia Jackson, the Modern Jazz Quartet, J. J. Johnson, Duke Ellington, Ahmad Jamal, and trumpeter and bandleader Maynard Ferguson. Folk artists included Pete Seeger, Richard Dyer-Bennet, and the Weavers. Reviews included the following comments. On the Maynard Ferguson Band: "some of the best jazz heard this year." On the Modern Jazz Quartet: "extraordinary." On Mahalia Jackson: "the world's greatest gospel singer." On J. J. Johnson: "first rate." On Duke Ellington: "truly a jazz concert . . . by a giant of jazz."[1]

In 1960, overwhelmed by the growth of their "little establishment," the Barbers decided to sell the Music Inn, together with its buildings and grounds, to a local entrepreneur, Don Soviero, but they retained their pet project, the School of Jazz, which they decided to house in the Wheatleigh mansion together with its faculty and students.

Financial difficulties almost caused the cancellation of the School in July, but at the last minute, Michael Bakwin, who was the owner of the Avaloch Inn (now the Apple Tree Inn), across the street from Tanglewood, and whose parents were among the founders of the Museum of Modern Art, gave the School a grant of

$5,000 "since an educational institution as significant in jazz and contemporary music as The School of Jazz must survive."[2] Following on this gift several other organizations and individuals contributed funds: the Zildjian cymbal company, United Artists, Associated Booking Corporation, the National Academy of Recording Arts and Sciences, the jazz critics Nat Hentoff and Ralph Gleason, the Music for Moderns music series from Milwaukee, Atlantic Records, BMI, Chappell Music Publishers, The Goldschmidt Foundation, Dizzy Gillespie, and Leonard Bernstein.

The members of the Modern Jazz Quartet, were, once again, on the faculty of the School of Jazz for 1960, as was Gunther Schuller. But several other crucial members of the faculty did not return.

Mahalia Jackson performs her joyful magic at the Music Barn, July 1959.

Bill Russo and Max Roach (trustees and faculty members since the founding of the School), Jim Hall (on the faculty since the beginning), Kenny Dorham (on the faculty since 1958), and Bill Evans (since 1959) did not teach at the School that summer. Herb Pomeroy, who had joined the faculty in 1958, only taught for one week, since he had arranged some engagements elsewhere with his own big band. Marshall Stearns, who had organized the very first symposium on jazz at the Music Inn in 1950 and had been one of the principal intellectual forces behind the founding of the School of Jazz, also did not return for the 1960 season. New to the teaching staff were J. J. Johnson, trombone; Earl Zindars, drums; Susan Freeman, bass; Ed Summerlin, saxophone; guests Freddie Hubbard,

trumpet, and John Garvey, who was a violist in the Walden String Quartet and professor of music at the University of Illinois. In residence were the Modern Jazz Quartet and the George Russell Sextet. The idea of adding string players to the roster (Garvey brought six string players to play in Lenox that summer) came from the movement known as "third stream music," for which Gunther Schuller was a prime mover. Schuller lived in both the jazz and the classical worlds, and he coined the term "third stream" in 1957.[3] The movement attempted to blend classical and jazz elements in the same composition and had been in existence for some time. Many interesting compositions resulted from it, including works by several of the musicians associated with the School of Jazz: J.J. Johnson, André Hodeir, Jimmy Giuffre, Bill Russo, Ran Blake, and Don Ellis, and especially John Lewis and Schuller himself. The idea of a "fusion" of the two styles had been discussed at a previous panel discussion at the Music Inn in 1956.[4] The movement itself has been controversial, as jazz purists believe that jazz has nothing to learn from classical music. But throughout its history jazz has leaned in the direction of the classical world in order to borrow some of its respectability.

Students that summer numbered 45 (including a saxophonist from Ceylon) out of a total of 300 applicants. Many of the students were already quite accomplished players. Newcomers to the school in 1960 who went on to careers in jazz were Jamey Aebersold, who played alto saxophone and became a leading publisher of jazz education books and recordings; Vera Auer, vibraphonist from Austria, who performed actively in her native country; Brian Cooke, who played French horn, viola, and piano and led an active career in music, performing, arranging, and composing; Michael Gibbs, trombonist from Rhodesia, who played in many bands and led his own; Don Heckman, alto saxophonist, who became a jazz journalist; Joe Hunt, drummer, who worked in many bands and taught at the Berklee College of Music; Chuck Israels, a highly regarded and widely recorded bassist, who played in Bill Evans's trio from 1961 until 1966 (and whose parents ran a classical-music summer camp in nearby Stockbridge); Steve Marcus, who played with Larry Coryell and led the Buddy Rich big band; Harold McKinney, pianist, well-known in Detroit; J. R. Monterose, tenor saxophonist, who recorded several albums; Jay Pruitt, trumpeter, who also worked as an arranger; and Dave Young, tenor saxophonist, who recorded with George Russell.

Among the evening lectures in 1960 was one on the relationship between jazz and contemporary (classical) music given by Gunther Schuller and another by the American composer Lukas Foss on non-jazz improvisation in small ensembles. Several lectures that year focused on the growing internationalization of jazz.

The final concert of the school featured traditional small jazz ensembles in the first half and "third-stream" works with jazz combos and strings in the second, including Bob Brookmeyer's "Champagne Blues" with J. J. Johnson on trombone, "Variants on a Theme of John Lewis" composed by Gunther Schuller (the theme was Lewis's "Django"), "Milano" by John Lewis, and "Piece for Guitar and Strings" by Jim Hall. A review of these works was lukewarm: "The numbers were interesting and pleasant but little more."[5] But they appeared on an album recorded by John Lewis later that year entitled *John Lewis Presents Contemporary Music - Jazz Abstractions* (Atlantic 1365).

The School must have faced considerable financial concerns in the fall, for a thirteen-page single-spaced typewritten document was produced, entitled "A Case for the School of Jazz," which appears to have been written by Stephanie Barber (there is an earlier draft in her hand), perhaps in conjunction with Philip Barber, Jules

Foster, and John Lewis. This was probably used as a fund-raising vehicle, for it ends with the sections "Current Needs of the School of Jazz" and "How You Can Help the School of Jazz." It begins with the following statement, which is both inspiring and revealing, for its appeal to "classical" authorities represents the continuing struggle of jazz for legitimacy even in the Fifties:

> Jazz has become within half a century the most important single force in American contemporary music both nationally and internationally. Audiences throughout Western Europe, Africa, and the Near East fill concert halls to overflowing to hear professional jazz groups [such] as the Modern Jazz Quartet and Louis Armstrong's band, and jazz soloists [such] as Sarah Vaughan and Benny Goodman play music which is uniquely and distinctly American. Conductors Bernstein, Mitropolous, and Ansermet, recognizing its value as the only distinctly American musical style, have encouraged its performance while composers [such] as Stravinsky, Hindemith, and scores of young Americans have realized some of jazz's improvisatory freedom and rhythms in their own compositions. Educators have begun to realize the importance of jazz to America's musical future, and such schools as the Universities of Indiana, Illinois, and California, Juilliard, and Brandeis have added either courses, workshops, or seminars to their curriculums to deal with the subject.
>
> However, in spite of its success in growth, jazz has needed the opportunity to build its own terminology, find mutual understanding among its professionals, and create its own educational methods – in short, the opportunity to crystallize as an art form. The School of Jazz is providing that opportunity.

Philanthropic opportunities provided by the document included the establishment of a "faculty chair," the contribution of a student scholarship, and (again mimicking Tanglewood) a "friends" system, which was divided into Patrons ($75 to $125), Sponsors ($50 to $74), Sustaining ($25 to $49), and Active ($10 to $24). Gifts were tax deductible.

In November of 1960, *Jazz Review* published "Two Reports on the School of Jazz," one by a faculty member, Gunther Schuller, and one by a student, Don Heckman. Schuller wrote that there was "a great need for the kind of finishing school that Lenox represents," that in Lenox "the young player, about to become professional, can

Students parading through the streets of Lenox.

learn much about his music and its presentation through personal, direct contact with some of the great names in jazz," and that "as long as the School at Lenox can contribute to the development of jazz on such a broad and catholic basis, its place in American musical life seems to me assured." Heckman singled out Schuller's history of jazz course for special praise: "Mr. Schuller was able to present one of the most interesting courses of the school session." He said that the school operates "in the most beautiful place imaginable." And he wrote: "I am happy to have attended the school at an early time in its history. It is an accomplished fact now and a force for the future."[6]

During the winter the Barbers sent out a newsletter from the School to its former students, trustees, and friends, providing news and gossip, and soliciting ideas for raising money. It announced that for 1961 the session would be expanded to four weeks. Also planned was relocation of the final faculty-student concert at the end of the session to a concert hall in New York. Encouraging news included the fact that a former part-time student had contributed $100 to the School, and the generous gesture of jazz writers Ralph Gleason and Nat Hentoff to donate to the School the income from two sets of their liner notes. "Friends" now numbered ten. "Perhaps some day we can approach Tanglewood's 10,000 Friends," hoped the newsletter. A happy announcement told readers that Percy Heath and his wife June had had a baby – a boy – whose name was Stuart Heath. His middle name was Wheatleigh. . . .[7]

Summary of School Achievements,
Music Inn in the Sixties,
Wheatleigh Hotel

Although an ambitious brochure was printed for the School of Jazz for 1961, the season never happened. The brochure announced a schedule that had expanded from three to four weeks and pictured a mixed-race ensemble in one photograph and a young and intense Gunther Schuller playing French horn in another. Scholarships were offered but, "due to the limited funds available to the School," they only represented $100 out of the tuition fee of $385. The faculty now included Artie Shaw, who had been in the audience for the previous year's final concert,[1] and was due to teach as "Instructor of Large Ensemble." But the financial problems that had dogged the School since its inception ultimately caused the 1961 season to be canceled and the School to close down. It had been "increasing its non-profits" year after year until it was no longer viable. "We never made any money," said Stephanie, "because we paid for everything, the food, the chef, the making of the beds."[2] Gunther Schuller thinks that the School failed because it was ahead of its time and "therefore it was not appreciated fully enough. The times were not ready for that sort of thing."[3] It is also possible that some of the members of the faculty were ready for a change or that their flourishing performing careers were taking them elsewhere in the summers. The Barbers had continued to use the same teachers for several years, but many of them were announced in the brochure as "on leave" for the 1961 session. These included Ray Brown, Kenny Dorham, Dizzy Gillespie, Jimmy Giuffre, Lee Konitz, Oscar Peterson, George Russell, and, for the first time since 1950, the very first lecturer at the Music Inn, Marshall Stearns.

The report of the dean of the School, Jules Foster, to the Governing Board, has a wistful air about it:

> During the four annual three-week sessions in Lenox, Massachusetts, 1957, 58, 59, 60, the School of Jazz has developed the first totally jazz oriented curriculum in the history of jazz. . . . The School has developed a high national and international reputation and has accepted a total of 155 students. Foreign students have attended from Africa, Austria, Sweden, Holland, India, Canada, Turkey, [and] Brazil, and American students have attended from 20 states. Under consideration for the 1961 season were students from Japan, Africa, and Yugoslavia. . . . Though $20,000 in scholarship aid has been administered to deserving students during the four sessions, it has been necessary for the school to refuse scholarship aid to the majority of students who apply. . . . That the School of Jazz has been able within its short history to achieve its primary goal of providing a pre-professional apprenticeship for the jazz musician is evidenced by the contributions of its alumni and faculty to the jazz field, not the least of which was

Ornette Coleman's New York debut in 1959. . . . But whether students enroll with an immediate goal in mind or for a less definitive reason, the impact of the experience on their lives has been visibly recognizable, and their continued correspondence with the school reflects its meaning. . . . Despite the school's positive achievements, the school has been unable because of the lack of adequate developmental funds to maintain a full-time year-round staff. This has severely limited the school's capacity for student recruitment, curriculum planning, and fund raising, and has, eventually forced the suspension of the annual session. . . . This report is respectfully submitted with my personal gratitude to those individuals and organizations who have, in spite of the difficulties, made four successful years possible.

During its four years of operation the School of Jazz had established a tradition of serious jazz study at a time when jazz was still fighting for acceptance as an art form. It had put black and white musicians, composers, performers and scholars together to learn from each other and make music together in the Berkshires – one of the most exclusive resort locations in the United States, one, moreover, that was a prestigious home of classical music for concertgoers. The Lenox School of Jazz provided a foundation in jazz music to 158 students,[4] many of whom went on to careers in jazz. It was the place where some of the most distinguished figures in American jazz, such as Ran Blake, Chuck Israels, David Baker, Don Ellis, Steve Kuhn, and Larry Ridley, first received their training in jazz, and where some, like Ornette Coleman and Don Cherry, were catapulted to public attention.

The Music Inn, founded by Philip and Stephanie Barber ten years earlier, inspired several compositions by jazz composers,

*Portrait of bassist
Percy Heath by Bruce
Mitchell.*

including John Lewis's "Fugue for Music Inn," Harold Farberman's *Music Inn Suite*, Dizzy Gillespie's "Wheatleigh Hall," Jimmy Giuffre's "Blues in the Barn," Margo Guryan's "Inn Tune," Dave Lahm's "The Potting Shed," J. J. Johnson's "Chip's Summer" (later renamed "Shuttlebug"), Fran Thorne's "Housatonic Huzzy," Arif Mardin's "Faculty Meeting," Edward ("Dizzy Sal") Saldanha's "Relaxin' at Music Inn," and Randy Weston's "Berkshire Blues." (Since the beginning Weston had occasionally attended events at Music Inn, while he worked at a hotel across town. In 1954 Stephanie Barber heard him alone at the piano one night and encouraged him to work at the Music Inn instead and to pursue a career in music. "Music Inn prepared me for my life," says Weston.)[5]

A number of art works were inspired by the Music Inn and those who worked there. In addition to the Jacob Lawrence watercolor from 1950 and a poster by Juanita Giuffre mentioned in the next chapter, the Viennese artist Sacha Kolin drew several illustrations for one of the Music Inn brochures.[6] In 1952 an exhibition entitled "Music in Art" was held at Music Inn, featuring two works by Kolin, "The Blues" and "Scherzo." Bruce Mitchell made some sketches of musicians at the Music Inn, and painted a wonderful portrait of Percy Heath (now in the possession of his widow, June Heath).[7] And the photographer Clemens Kalischer, who immigrated to the United States as a refugee from Nazi Germany and ultimately settled in Stockbridge, made several photographs of scenes in and around the Inn. Warren Fowler, a photojournalist, made a very large number of photographs at the Inn over its lifetime, including the delightful shot of Stephanie Barber with Louis Armstrong in 1957. (In 1996 the Berkshire Museum Camera Club established an annual Warren Fowler Memorial Award to honor the photographer. For many years Fowler edited the Dave Brubeck Newsletter.) An abstract painting of Percy Heath at the Inn by Springfield artist Lou Stovall was displayed at the Music Barn in 1958. (It was stolen from the exhibit that August.)

The Music Inn and its assorted spin-offs – the roundtables, the folk and jazz festivals, the Music Barn concerts, the Potting Shed nightclub, Concerts for Connoisseurs, the residencies, the School of Jazz – were unique for a combination of qualities: the performers, lecturers, and scholars were resident; guests could mingle with the musicians; and students could mingle with the stars. "It was really in some respects like being on shipboard," said Nat Hentoff, jazz critic and journalist and editor of Down Beat. "Because there were really no delimitations as to hours or place, in terms of when you could talk to musicians and when they could talk to each other. It was a continuous flow, extraordinarily relaxed, and that's what made it different."[8] And Dave Brubeck remarked, "Jazz has often been associated with a city. . . . But it can happen wherever the right guys get together. And a lot was happening up in Lenox. . . . [T]he boundaries of jazz were being stretched."[9]

Countless other non-jazz musicians of all kinds also passed through the Music Inn in the Fifties. In addition to the many folk singers already mentioned, the roster included the West Indian dancer, singer, and actor Geoffrey Holder; Israeli singer Martha Schlamme;[10] and the Nigerian drummer named Babatunde Olatunji, who taught about African drumming and worked his way through a Ph.D. at New York University by teaching and performing. He was at Music Inn for several years and released his most famous recording *Drums of Passion* in 1959.[11] The satirical singer and pianist Tom Lehrer was a popular favorite for three years at the Music Barn. The Four Freshmen, an a-capella group; calypso singers; the Lord Burgess Troupe from Jamaica; the Eva Jessye Choir; and barbershop quartets such as the Buffalo Bills, the Valley Four, and the Clip Chords: all these appeared on the stage of the Music Barn in Lenox.

Don Soviero, the entrepreneur who bought the Music Inn from the Barbers in 1960, expanded the audience capacity of the Music Barn out onto the lawn to accommodate five or six thousand people. Some of the same jazz performers continued to play there, but in keeping with the spirit of the times, the folk and proto-rock acts began to get more famous: Joan Baez, Carly Simon, Bob Dylan, and Don McLean all appeared at the Lenox venue in the early Sixties. In 1967 Soviero went bankrupt. Reopening under new ownership in 1970, the new Music Inn became a smaller Woodstock, and it included shops, an art gallery, a movie theater, and a bar with live music.[12] Performers such as Arlo Guthrie, the Byrds, Taj Mahal, Bob Marley, Van Morrison, Bruce Springsteen, the Kinks, the Allman Brothers, Tina Turner, Bonnie Raitt, and Ravi Shankar all performed in the new open setting during the Seventies. But the noise and the crowds began to be too much for the rural Berkshires. Town officials claimed that 15,000 people attended the concert by The Outlaws in 1979. One neighbor, Nate Horwith, complained for years about the noise at the concerts. And, colorfully, he compared the intrusion of the noise coming from the concerts to "someone coming into your hospital room in the middle of the night and giving you an enema because they thought it was someone else's room."[13] Unable to obtain enforcement of noise ordinances from local politicians, Horwith sold his house and his land. The place started to resemble a circus, with impromptu stage acts, motorcycle gangs, drugged out audiences, and people hanging from the tension lines. A Stockbridge selectman recalled "the condition of the place was atrocious. Fences were bent over, and grass hadn't been cut, and urinals hadn't been cleaned."[14] And Tanglewood itself, with an eye to profits, began to compete by hosting popular music concerts at the hallowed ground of classical propriety. In 1979, after an Allman Brothers concert at Music Inn at which a crowd of concert-goers decided to storm the gate and were met by members of the "security" forces wielding clubs, sending several of them to hospital, the Music Inn closed its doors for the last time. The local newspaper described the new scene as "totally incompatible" with the atmosphere of the Berkshires.[15]

Philip and Stephanie Barber continued to run Wheatleigh as

a hotel through the 1960s ("After the School of Jazz, we were just innkeepers," said Stephanie),[16] and many celebrities stayed there, including conductors such as Leonard Bernstein and Erich Leinsdorf; actors like Anne Bancroft, Anne Jackson, and Eli Wallach; playwrights such as Eugene Ionesco and John Guare; singer Joan Baez; and at one time the Princess of Japan. Philip and Stephanie were separated in 1972. Stephanie and her two children (her sons Chip and Hillary) continued to live at Wheatleigh, where she also ran a small informal lounge called *La Cave* (where she herself also used to sing), and, for a time, a music theater known as the Lenox Arts Center produced shows there as well. After the separation Stephanie supplemented her income by becoming a real estate broker, with many celebrities such as Eric Erickson and Norman Mailer among her clients.

Amusingly, the figure of Stephanie Barber turns up in a memoir by Stephen Citron and Anne Edwards, which describes an inn they started in the Berkshires in the early Seventies. One evening, Citron writes, a reservation came in for a Mrs. Barber.

> Stephanie Barber was a legend in Berkshire County. She sang, ran an elegant inn, held a real estate license, and was well known for her flamboyant costumes. She had previously owned Music Inn and had been responsible for bringing, among others, Billie Holiday to the area. If she liked [our inn] it could be a start. . . . I went to greet [them]. There was no doubt in my mind which woman was Stephanie Barber. She had been described to me as always being costumed, never just dressed. All eyes in the room were on [this] regal blonde lady wearing a white satin gown and carrying a black ostrich-feather fan. . . . [After dinner], leaning over and kissing me on the cheek, she said, "Welcome to the Berkshires, *cheri*."[17]

Stephanie's Future,
Reminiscences and Evaluations
of the School's Significance

In 1975 Dizzy Gillespie and the members of the Modern Jazz Quartet gave a concert as a present to Stephanie at Wheatleigh under the aegis of the Lenox Arts Center. The concert was billed as a twentieth-anniversary celebration of the founding of the School of Jazz, although, as we have seen, the School was in fact established in 1957.[1] The concert was sold out at 120 people in the small concert hall at Wheatleigh and was introduced by Gunther Schuller, who described it as a "remembrance of things past."[2] In 1976, Stephanie Barber sold the mansion and moved to a smaller house in Lenox. She continued to sing occasionally and once gave a show at Alice's, a restaurant at the Avaloch Inn. A fine poster for this performance (July 17, 1977) was painted by Juanita Giuffre, the artist and wife of Jimmy Giuffre. It shows the singer in a stylish hat and cape, with emphasis on her large eyes, and it gives off the atmosphere of the French fin-de-siècle posters she and her husband used to collect.[3] (The concert was actually advertised on a lighted marquee in New York City's Times Square. Stephanie had won the use of the marquee in a raffle sponsored by the Manhattan Theatre Club.) In 1972 Philip Barber moved to Becket, Massachusetts, a small town only ten miles or so from Lenox, where he founded the Becket Arts Center (which still has a Philip Barber Gallery) and married for the fifth time. He died in 1981. Stephanie was remarried in 1989 to Arthur Collins, a professor of English at the State University of New York at Albany. She died in 2003 at the age of 84, leaving her second husband, two sons (Chip and Hillary), three stepsons, three stepdaughters, fifteen grandchildren and one great-grandchild. At the memorial service, two former students of the School of Jazz – Ran Blake and Dick Katz – and one of the members of the faculty – Percy Heath – performed; as did Tom Lehrer, who had become a lifelong friend of Stephanie's after appearing at the Music Barn several times; and recordings of Ravel's "Pavane for a Dead Princess" and Armstrong's "What A Wonderful World" were played. Her second husband, Arthur Collins, told the local paper that nobody had ever had a bad word to say about her. Her famous collection of hats was auctioned off for charity in the spring of 2004.

In an undated typescript Philip Barber wrote a brief reminiscence of "The Concerts at Music Inn: Before the Great Controversy." He recalls the earliest days of the Inn when at the first concert "no one came. Not one person. Only the guests and staff heard a really memorable concert." He relates the story of visiting jazz guitarist Danny Barker, who made his first instrument from strips of rubber cut from an old inner tube and "nailed to the barn door at varying tensions." He relates some delightful anecdotes, including one about Count Basie joining the Barbers for a drink after one of his appearances. He asked for a gin. "Gin and what?" asked Barber.

*Poster for a concert by
Stephanie Barber, painted
by Juanita Giuffre, 1977.*

"Gin and a glass," replied Basie.

Another story tells of how Sarah Vaughan, who was already late for her appearance at the Music Barn, was getting ready in the Barbers' house on the grounds immediately before her concert:

> On the couch was three-and-a-half-year-old Chip Barber,
>   very disconsolate.
> "What's wrong, sweetheart?" she asked him.
> "They won't let me stay up for your concert."
> "Never mind. I'll sing you a special concert."
> And she did, while a thousand people waited in the
>   Music Barn theater.

Barber also tells of how in 1956 they had only a very small bar with an amateur bartender. Eddie Condon was there after his concert, very thirsty. After waiting for a very long time to get served, he said to the bartender: "You're a piano player, aren't you?" Delighted, the young Juilliard student said, "Why, yes. But how did you know?" Condon replied, "I knew damn well you weren't a bartender!"

Philip Barber also discusses the reasoning behind the opening of Music Barn:

> So by economics we were driven to our next step – converting the courtyard and lower floor of the huge haybarn into a thousand-seat concert hall and stage. . . . Now we could bring musicians and groups well known enough to draw hundreds of the public and so pay for our expenses. . . . At first we found it difficult to book attractions. . . . Agents then regarded jazz as something played in night clubs in twenty-minute "sets" or by big bands in large dance halls, and they thought our idea was a crazy one. . . . We ended [that first] season with a modest profit.

Barber gives as an example the box office figures for the 1957 season: attendance 15,414; receipts $37,723. He does not list the expenses. He concludes the story by lamenting the current obsession with profits. "At Music Inn in the Fifties we were able to consider first of all, 'Will it be interesting and enjoyable?' And it was – to musicians, to audience, and to me."

The last word may contain a clue as to why the typescript was not published. For it was sent to the *Berkshire Eagle*, but publication was refused, reportedly on the grounds that in the twelve pages Philip Barber had made no mention of the contributions to the Music Inn of his former wife Stephanie.

Jimmy Giuffre performed at Wheatleigh during the 1980s with

a group he called The Jimmy Giuffre 4, with Pete Levin, keyboards; Bob Nieske, electric bass; and Randy Kaye, percussion. John Lewis returned to Lenox in 1996 to play at a fundraising concert for the Lenox Library with Wynton Marsalis. The Library asked Stephanie Barber to phone John Lewis with the request for him to play. That was all it took, said Lewis. "She has done so much for jazz. She's a wonderful person, remarkably wonderful."[4] Lewis recalled his time at Music Inn: "We were invited by the Barbers to come up to be the quartet in residence. It was a wonderful experience, quite unique. I'd never heard of any other jazz group invited for something like that."[5] At the memorial service for John Lewis, who died in 2001, the critic Gary Giddins gave away the secret of his success as a musician, leader, and one of the founders of the School of Jazz: "He was a gentle man, but he also had that steely resolve. I never saw him raise his voice, but I never saw him not get what he wanted."[6]

At least two books about Music Inn have been contemplated but never came to fruition. In 1987 journalist Eileen Kuperschmid interviewed Stephanie Barber with an eye to producing a book about her, but this did not materialize. At about this same time Jules Foster and Stephanie also planned a book of photographs relating to Music Inn. This would have been entitled *A Photographic Memoir of Music Inn*, but a publisher was not found.[7] In 1995, Seth Rogovoy, a Berkshire journalist and arts critic, published a magazine article about the Music Inn.[8] He asked Stephanie for her cooperation on a book, but she declined the request and wrote to him that her legal counsel suggested she urge him "not to continue with the contemplated project at this time."[9] This was probably because the Barber/Foster project was still in the works, for the following statement was placed alongside Rogovoy's article when it appeared on the web: "A book, *A Photographic Memoir of Music Inn*, is in process, authored by Stephanie Barber, Music Inn

*Crowds gathering for the problematic Kingston Trio
concert at the Music Barn, July 1959.*

founder, with J. Foster, Berkshire Music Barn manager and School
of Jazz dean. The volume documents the development of the Inn,
Barn and School from 1950 and includes Stephanie Barber's personal memoirs; historic photographs by Clemens Kalischer, Warren
D. Fowler and others; and contributions from major artists who
participated in Music Inn activities."[10] A book that was to include a
chapter on the Music Inn was announced in 1998 by John Gennari,
an English professor. It has not yet been published.[11] And a short
article on the Music Inn was published by Richard Houdek in 2006
in *Berkshire Home Style* magazine.[12] The *New Grove Dictionary of
Jazz* has no entries on the Lenox School of Jazz or the Music Inn.
Neither the *New Grove Dictionary of Music and Musicians* nor the
New Grove Dictionary of American Music has entries relating to the
School of Jazz.

In 1987, for the thirtieth anniversary of the School, Jules Foster, who had been the School's dean, intended to stage a reunion of some of the original faculty and students, organize an anniversary concert, and produce a documentary film for cable television. This project did not materialize.

Research on the School of Jazz was posted on the web in 1993 by Michael Fitzgerald, who said: "[T]he quantity, quality, and stature of the teachers [at Lenox] has never been equaled."[13]

In 1998, a tribute to Stephanie Barber and to Music Inn was produced by the National Music Foundation in Lenox with the idea of establishing a permanent archive of materials relating to Music Inn. The event was a joyful celebration of the achievements of the Music Inn and of the School of Jazz. Dave and Iola Brubeck were there, as were Bill Russo, Percy Heath, and Randy Weston. Written tributes were sent by Ahmet Ertegun, John Lewis, Jimmy and Juanita Giuffre, and Nat Hentoff.[14] After dinner Sonny Rollins played a concert dedicated to Stephanie. However no archive for the materials was established at the National Music Foundation, which departed Lenox not long afterwards. Arthur Collins, Stephanie Barber's second husband, and Stephanie's sons and stepsons ultimately donated their archive to the Lenox Library Association, where it is being held for research and reference.

In September 2004 the Jazz Journalists Association hosted a panel discussion about the Music Inn and the state of jazz in New England at the Tanglewood Jazz Festival. Among the panelists were Benjamin Barber and Dave and Iola Brubeck. At this event Stephanie Barber was posthumously awarded an "Unsung Hero" award by the New England Jazz Alliance for her "selfless promotion of jazz as an art form through her establishment of Music Inn and the School of Jazz at Lenox."[15]

At this time work is underway to produce another documentary film about the Music Inn. One of the co-producers is George Schuller, Gunther Schuller's son, who is also planning a CD set gathering together recordings from the Music Inn. The film is to include a reunion and feature dozens of interviews with surviving students and teachers of the school as well as a narrative by Benjamin Barber.[16] The producer, Ben Barenholtz, used to run a movie theater on the grounds of the Music Inn in the Seventies. Filmmaker Casey Meade, who is the son of David Rothstein, the third owner of the Music Inn in the Seventies, and of Nancy Fitzpatrick, who still lives in the renovated Potting Shed, said about the project: "The knowledge of the Music Inn has fallen out of the present consciousness. I think a lot of people are going to be very surprised and interested. It was a very important destination (for jazz and folk musicians alike) at the time and was important in the historical development of the music."[17]

When Sonny Rollins played in Lenox in 1998, he said, "I remember [Music Inn] as a very futuristic place in that it presented the jazz musicians in a very dignified setting. There was a real atmosphere of scholarship and dignity . . . There's no place quite like it now."[18] And in a recent interview he told me that the Lenox School of Jazz

> was a nice respite from the usual jazz itineraries. There seemed to be a great respect for the music – something that was not always the case in the places we were used to. The importance of the School of Jazz was that it gave jazz an air of respectability that was unknown at that time. That was the most important thing."[19]

Ed Bride, the Vice President of the New England Jazz Alliance, says of the historical position of the School of Jazz:

Before the Newport Jazz Festival, there was Music Inn and its fabled Berkshire Music Barn; and before almost any other school there was the School of Jazz at Lenox. Both of these operations succeeded in making life more interesting for jazz lovers. With its renowned instructors from the jazz world, the School of Jazz at Lenox is recalled even today by former students and faculty alike as a significant period in the development of jazz. History was made there, to say nothing of the music.[20]

Former student David Baker discussed the significance of the School of Jazz in 2002, when he was elected to the presidency of the International Association of Jazz Educators. He was interviewed by Darius Brubeck, Dave and Iola's oldest son, who first met David Baker in Lenox when he was twelve years old and his father was in residence at the School. In part the interview went as follows:

> BRUBECK: I think the hipness of that period was [very deep]. People had to be where they could learn from each other and influence each other to make the 1960s happen. The '60s began in 1959, and the discussions I have been having not only suggest a time but a place – and the place looks like Lenox.
> BAKER: I would say so. It was the first organized jazz educational situation I'd ever been in. To have all of these people in the same place – [I said to myself:] "Now grab it!" . . . So all of these ideas were in the air, kind of the zeitgeist, and all of a sudden . . . Lenox, man, it was *alive!*[21]

Randy Weston, who spent ten summers in the Berkshires, says that the School of Jazz was "so important in bringing people together. It was in incredible experience for all of us. We were all treated

The new condominiums on the site of the Music Inn have preserved the distinctive cupola and weather vane from the 1950s.

with respect and dignity. We were all totally involved in culture and beauty and music and love."[22]

And Gunther Schuller, composer, scholar, educator, and fount of energy at Lenox, who went on to start the first degree-granting program in jazz in the late Sixties when he was president of the New England Conservatory, is still passionate about what was accomplished at Lenox:

> The Lenox School of Jazz was an incredible, unique, pioneering effort in the teaching of jazz. It was twenty years ahead of its time, so it wasn't appreciated fully enough. It had master teachers – the cream of the crop – and no commercialism. At Tanglewood, Koussevitsky had created a place for students that was an incredible, visionary sanctuary – pure, and unrelated to the *business* of music. That was our model. You didn't do that in those days. You went on the road. There *were* no schools. Even at Indiana University there was a fantastic jazz band that had to rehearse in the basement. Jazz wasn't allowed upstairs! And it certainly wasn't in the curriculum. The Lenox School of Jazz was absolutely unique.[23]

The outbuildings of the Music Inn have been converted to condominiums, and the Wheatleigh mansion, having undergone extensive restoration, is now a fine hotel and restaurant. But the rooms of these buildings as well as the fields and stone fences of the property have witnessed a lot of history, including a vital and formative chapter in the history of American jazz, not to mention the history of America's soul.

APPENDIX 1: RECORDINGS MADE WHOLLY OR
IN PART AT THE MUSIC INN

The Modern Jazz Quartet at Music Inn, Guest Artist: Jimmy Giuffre.
Recorded August 28, 1956.
John Lewis (piano), Milt Jackson (vibraphone), Percy Heath (bass), Connie
Kay (drums); Jimmy Giuffre (clarinet).
Atlantic 1247; Warner Music Japan MTCJ-6005 (WQCP-214) (CD).

Historic Jazz Concert at Music Inn. Recorded August 30, 1956.
Jimmy Giuffre (clarinet and tenor saxophone), Pee Wee Russell (clarinet),
Rex Stewart (trumpet), Herbie Mann (flute), Teddy Charles (vibraphone),
Dick Katz (piano), George Wein (piano), Percy Heath (bass), Oscar Pettiford
(bass and cello), Ray Brown (bass), Connie Kay (drums).
Atlantic 1298.

The Modern Jazz Quartet and Guests: Third Stream Music. "Da Capo" and
"Fine." Recorded August 24, 1957.
John Lewis (piano), Milt Jackson (vibraphone), Percy Heath (bass), Connie
Kay (drums); Jimmy Giuffre (clarinet).
Atlantic 1345; Wounded Bird Records WOU 1345 (CD).

*Max Roach with the Boston Percussion Ensemble under the Direction of Har-
old Farberman.*
Recorded August 17, 1958.
Max Roach (drums) and members of the Boston Symphony Orchestra (Har-
old Farberman, conductor).
Mercury MG 36144.

The Modern Jazz Quartet at Music Inn, Guest Artist: Sonny Rollins.
Recorded August 31, 1958.
John Lewis (piano), Milt Jackson (vibraphone), Percy Heath (bass), Connie
Kay (drums); Sonny Rollins (tenor saxophone).
Atlantic 1299; Mobile Fidelity 632 (CD); Collectables Jazz Classics COL
CD 7785 (CD).

Jimmy Giuffre: The Four Brothers Sound.
Recorded September 1, 1958.
Jimmy Giuffre (tenor saxophones), Bob Brookmeyer (piano), Jim Hall (guitar).
Atlantic 1295; Collectables Jazz Classics COL CD 6284 (CD).

Ornette Coleman, Don Cherry, Kenny Dorham – Lenox School of Jazz Concert.
"The Sphinx" and "Inn Tune."
Recorded August 29, 1959.
Ornette Coleman (alto saxophone), Don Cherry (pocket trumpet), Kent Mc-Garity (trombone), Steve Kuhn (piano), Ron Brown (piano), Larry Ridley (bass), Barry Greenspan (drums).
Royal Jazz SOJ 1/2, RJD 513 (CD).

APPENDIX 2: THE ORIGINAL CHARTER OF THE LENOX SCHOOL OF JAZZ

The School of Jazz, Inc., is a non-profit organization chartered under the laws of the State of Massachusetts.
The purpose of the School of Jazz, Inc., is to teach and to foster the study of jazz in all its aspects, including its techniques of expression, its improvisation and its composition; also its history, origin, its international development and its relationship to other arts; to provide for individual instruction as well as rehearsal in both large ensemble and in small groups, and to develop for its students the experience of playing for public audiences.

APPENDIX 3: FROM THE LINER NOTES TO THE RECORDING *HISTORIC JAZZ CONCERT AT MUSIC INN* (Atlantic 1298) BY NAT HENTOFF

This instantaneous concert . . . took place on August 30, 1956 toward the end of a unique experience in jazz history. The concert was recorded at the Music Barn, a tent-theatre . . . on the grounds of the Music Inn in the Berkshires in Lenox, Massachusetts. . . . For five days, a number of jazz musicians of widely varying ages and "schools" were invited . . . to sit and discuss for as long as seemed necessary specific jazz subjects. . . . It's difficult to verbalize how stimulating that week was. . . . [T]he mutual affection and warmth was exhilaratingly contagious, and it was this experience that led directly to the decision by the Barbers and John Lewis to form the School of Jazz at Music Inn.

APPENDIX 4: FROM "A LETTER FROM LENOX, MASSACHUSETTS," *JAZZ REVIEW*, OCTOBER 1959, BY MARTIN WILLIAMS

August 31, 1959. From the first day of this year's session of the School of Jazz there was undeniably something in the air, and it was not long before one realized exactly what it was: in its third year the School was coming of age. It was probably possible in past summers to overhear a student bull session on whether life or art is more important, but it would hardly have seemed so appropriate – and for most of the people involved this year they were really the same thing. . . . One could say that of jazz itself – and in our time one can say it of few other human activities. There were several reasons for this new atmosphere at Lenox, but as one reflects on them, he realizes they don't explain it all. The mysterious and natural process of growth is simply a part of it – and perhaps the mysticism of 3 is too.

APPENDIX 5: 1959 LENOX SCHOOL OF JAZZ
FINAL CONCERT PROGRAM

THE SCHOOL OF JAZZ, INCORPORATED
presents
THE THIRD ANNUAL BENEFIT CONCERT
August 29, 1959 – 8:30 P.M.
BERKSHIRE MUSIC BARN
LENOX, MASSACHUSETTS

PROGRAM

Straight No Chaser (Thelonious Monk)
Aristocracy (Sandy Schmidt)
Lone Ranger and the Great Horace Silver (David Baker)
Song for Gunther (David Baker)

Gunther Schuller Ensemble: Perry Robinson-cl; John Eckert-tpt; Don
Stewart-tsx; David Baker-btbn; Gunther Schuller-fr hn; Sandy Schmidt,
Nico Bunink-p; Mona Neves-b; Bob Fuhlrodt-d

Monk's Sphere (Gary McFarland)
Summer Day (Gary McFarland)
Relaxin' At Music Inn (Dizzy Sal)
Jingles (Wes Montgomery, arr. Al Kiger)

Bill Evans, Jim Hall, Connie Kay Ensemble: Al Kiger-tpt; Ted Casher-tsx;
Dick Wright-tbn; Gary McFarland-vbs; Attilla Zoller-g; Dizzy Sal-p; Doug
McLaughlin-b; Bill Sharfman-d

Vanguard (Ran Blake)
Softly, As in a Morning Sunrise (Oscar Hammerstein & Sigmund Romberg)
Milano (John Lewis)
D. C. Special (Kenny Dorham)

Kenny Dorham Ensemble: Peter Farmer, Kenny Dorham-tpt; Sture Swenson-
bsx, tsx; Paul Dunyhower-tbn; David Lahm, Ran Blake-p; Walter Bernard-b;
John Bergamo-d

The Sphinx (Ornette Coleman)
Compassion (Ornette Coleman)
Giggin' (Ornette Coleman)
Inn Tune (Margo Guryan)

Max Roach, John Lewis Ensemble: Don Cherry-tpt; Ornette Coleman-asx; Kent McGarity-tbn, btpt; Steve Kuhn, Ron Brown-p; Larry Ridley-b; Barry Greenspan-d

INTERMISSION

Red (Jimmy Giuffre)
Stratusphunk (George Russell)
Come Rain or Come Shine (Harold Arlen & Johnny Mercer)
Ray's Time (Jimmy Giuffre)

Jimmy Giuffre F. & M. Schaefer Scholarship Ensemble: Tony Greenwald-tpt; Jimmy Giuffre-ww; Ian Underwood-f; Lenny Popkin-asx; Herb Gardner-tbn; David Mackay-p; John Keyser-b; Paul Cohen-d

To Thee, O Asphodel (Bobby Freedman)
Domingo (Benny Golson)
Take the A Train (Billy Strayhorn)
Sweet and Lovely
Paul's Pal (Sonny Rollins)
Blue Grass (Danny Kent)

Herb Pomeroy Ensemble: Tony Greenwald, Al Kiger, 2 unknown-tpt; Ornette Coleman, Lenny Popkin-asx; Ian Underwood-f, asx; Ted Casher-tsx; Sture Swenson-bsx?; Herb Gardner, Paul Dunyhower?-tbn; David Baker-btbn; Gary McFarland-vibes; David Mackay-p; John Keyser-b; Paul Cohen-d; Herb Pomeroy-cond

BIBLIOGRAPHY

BOOKS AND ARTICLES

Allen, Donald, ed. *Composed on the Tongue*. Bolinas, California: Grey Fox, 1980.

Anon. "Beret and Goatee to Play 2d Fiddle to Cap and Gown as Jazz Goes to School," *Variety* (February 6, 1957), 49; *Jazz Today*, May, 1957.

Anon. "Jazz Swings at Music Inn Jazz School," *Metronome*, July, 1957.

Anon. "Jazz without Juleps." *Newsweek*, September 1, 1958.

Anon. [Mr. Harper.] "Jumping Juilliard." *Harper's Magazine*, November, 1957, 82-3.

Anon. "Lenox Gets a Head," *Down Beat* (March 19, 1959), 9.

Anon. "Music Inn: They Come to Play." *Business Week*, September 19, 1953.

Anon. "Profs with a Purpose," *Down Beat* (July 10, 1958), 9.

Anon. "Report on Lenox," *Down Beat* (October 15, 1959), 11.

Anon. "The Berkshires: Sports, Scenery, and Culture, Too." *Cue*, Spring, 1953.

Anon. "The Composer in Jazz: More Time for Deep Thought," *Jazz Today*, December, 1956.

Anon. "The Lenox School of Jazz," *Down Beat* (November 13, 1958), 20.

Anon. "The Lenox School of Jazz," *Jazz Education Journal* 35 (2002): 48-51.

Anon. "The School at Lenox," *Down Beat* (November 10, 1960), 13.

Anon. "The School of Jazz," *Down Beat* (October 3, 1957), 23.

Anon. "The School of Jazz: A Practical Approach to Music Education." *Metronome*, October, 1958.

Anon. "The School of Jazz, Part II: A Practical Approach to Music Education." *Metronome*, November, 1958.

Barber, Philip Willson. *The Scene Technician's Handbook*. New York: Whitlock, 1928.

Brookmeyer, Bob. "The School of Jazz: Faculty Views." *Jazz Review*, February, 1959.

Brubeck, Darius. "David Baker and the Lenox School of Jazz." *Jazz Education Journal*, September, 2002.

Bryan, Clark W. *The Book of Berkshire, Describing and Illustrating its Hills and Homes, and Telling Where They Are, What They Are and Why They*

Are Destined to Become the Most Charming and Desirable Summer Homes in America. For the Season of 1887. Reprint: North Egremont, Massachusetts: Past Perfect, 1993.

Claxton, William and Joachim E. Berendt. *Jazz Life*. Offenburg: Burda, 1961.

Coss, Paul D. "Barn Dance in Lenox That's Something Else," *Metronome* (September, 1955), 8.

DeVeaux, Scott. Review of *Miles: The Autobiography*. In *American Music* 10 (1992), 93.

Edwards, Anne and Stephen Citron. *The Inn and Us*. New York: Random House, 1976.

Feather, Leonard. *The Book of Jazz: A Guide to the Entire Field*. New York: Horizon, 1957.

Finkelstein, Sidney. *Jazz: A People's Music*. New York: Citadel, 1948.

Frazier, George. "The Story of Jazz." *Coronet*, March, 1959.

Gennari, John. *Blowin' Hot and Cool: Jazz and Its Critics*. Chicago: Chicago University Press, 2006.

Gillespie, Dizzy. *To Be, or Not . . . to Bop*. New York: Da Capo, 1985.

Ginsberg, Allen. "Howl." In *Collected Poems, 1947-1980*. New York: Harper and Row, 1984.

Hentoff, Nat. "A Civilian's Report: Jazz Scholarships, Anyone?" *Metronome*, December, 1957.

Hentoff, Nat. "Counterpoint," *Down Beat* (June 1, 1955), 25.

_____. "Not So Random, Not So Festive Thoughts." *Jazz Today*, October, 1957.

_____, "The Tanglewood Jazz School," *Saturday Review* (September 14, 1957), 66.

Hobson, Wilder. "The Amen Corner: Soft Airs." *Saturday Review*, May, 1959.

Robert M. Hodesh, "The Musical Berkshires: 'Biggest Summer Culture Foundry in the Country'," *Lincoln-Mercury Times*, May-June, 1955.

Holmes, John Clellon. "The Golden Age: Time Present." *Esquire*, January, 1959.

Kerouac, Jack. "Jazz of the Beat Generation." In *New World Writing* 7. New York: New American Library, 1955.

Kerouac, Jack. *On the Road*. New York: Viking, 1957.

Leon, Stephen. "The Day the Music Died." *Berkshires Week*, August 23-29, 1985.

Litweiler, John. *The Freedom Principle: Jazz after 1958*. New York: William Morrow, 1984.

Luhan, Mabel Dodge. *Intimate Memories*. New York: Harcourt, Brace, [1933].

Maher, Jack. "The School of Jazz: Amazing Talent Marks Third Year." *Metronome*, October, 1959.

Mailer, Norman. "The White Negro: Superficial Reflections on the Hipster." *Dissent* 4/3 (Summer 1957), 276-93.

Maren, Roger. "A Few False Notes at Newport." *The Reporter*, September 8, 1955.

Meltzer, David, ed. *Reading Jazz*. San Francisco: Mercury, 1993.

O'Hara, Frank. *Collected Poems*. New York: Knopf, 1972.

A Pride of Palaces: Lenox Summer Cottages 1883-1933: Sixty Photographs by Edwin Hale Lincoln 1848-1938, ed. Donald T. Oakes. Lenox, Massachusetts: The Lenox Library Association, 1981.

Pynchon, Thomas. *V*. Philadelphia: Lippincott, 1963.

Reisner, Robert. "Reminiscences of Marshall Stearns." *Journal of Jazz Studies* 1 (1973), 84-9.

Riddle, Ron. "A Look Back at Lenox." *Jazz: A Quarterly of American Music*. October, 1958.

Robinson, Perry and Florence Wetzel. *Perry Robinson: The Traveler* (Lincoln, Nebraska: Writers Club, 2002).

_____, "The School of Jazz in Lenox, Massachusetts." *Coda* (July/August 2002): 7-9.

Rogovoy, Seth. "For Jazzmen Lewis and Marsalis, It's a Lifelong Affair with Lenox." *Berkshires Week*, October 10, 1996, 12-13.

_____. "The Life and Times of Music Inn." *Berkshire Magazine*, Summer, 1995.

Sargeant, Winthrop. *Jazz Hot and Hybrid*. New York: Arrow, 1948.

Saussy, F. Tupper. *Rulers Of Evil*. New York: HarperCollins, 1999.

_____. *The Miracle on Main Street: Saving Yourself and America from Financial Ruin*. 6th ed. Sewanee, Tennessee: Spencer Judd, 1984.

Schuller, Gunther and Don Heckman. "Two Reports on the School of Jazz."

Jazz Review, November, 1960, 14.

Schwerin, Jules. *Got to Tell It: Mahalia Jackson, Queen of Gospel*. New York: Oxford University Press, 1992.

Shipton, Alyn. *A New History of Jazz*. London: Continuum, 2001.

Spellman, A. B. *Four Lives in the Bebop Business*. [London]: MacGibbon and Kee, 1967.

Stearns, Marshall and Jean. *Jazz Dance: The Story of American Vernacular Dance*. Reprint: New York: Da Capo, 1994.

Stephens, Lorin. "An Interview with Jimmy Giuffre: The Passionate Conviction." *Jazz Review*, February, 1960.

Taubman, Howard. "Country Jazz," *New York Times*, August 7, 1955.

de Toledano, Ralph. *Frontiers of Jazz*. New York: Durrell, 1947

Ulanov, Barry. "Women in Jazz: Do They Belong?" *Down Beat* (January 9, 1958), 17.

Williams, Martin. "A Letter from Lenox, Mass." *Jazz Review*, October 1959.

WEBSITES

All About Jazz. "Modern Jazz Quartet: The Music Inn." http://www. allaboutjazz.com/php/article.php?id=454. (Accessed July 15, 2005.)

Fitzgerald, Michael. "The Lenox School of Jazz." http://www.jazzdiscography.com/Lenox/lenhome.htm. (Accessed June 28, 2005.)

NFO.net. "American Big Bands Database Plus." http://nfo.net/usa/b7.htm. (Accessed June 22, 2005.)

Projectile Arts. "Music Inn: A Documentary Film." http://www.projectilearts.org/musicinn/history/founders.html. (Accessed June 16, 2005.)

Rogovoy, Seth. "Music Foundation to Honor Music Inn Legacy and Founder Stephanie Barber." http://www.berkshireweb.com/rogovoy/ interviews/barber.html. (Accessed July 21, 2005.)

The Beat Page. "John Clennon Holmes." http://www.rooknet.com/ beatpage/writers/holmes.html. (Accessed September 27, 2004.)

INTERVIEWS

[unless otherwise stated, all interviews were conducted by the author]

Barber, Benjamin. [Benjamin Barber interview.] West Stockbridge, Massachusetts, July to August, 2005.

Barber, Stephanie. [Stephanie Barber interview.] "Chanson de Stephanie." Unpublished interview with Stephanie Barber by Jules Foster. Lenox, Massachusetts. August 18, 1995.

Barber, Stephanie and Arthur Collins. [Barber/Collins interview.] Unpublished interview with Stephanie Barber and Arthur Collins by Eileen Kuperschmid. Lenox, Massachusetts. October 27, 1987.

Coleman, Ornette. [Ornette Coleman interview.] New York City, June 29, 2005.

Collins, Arthur. [Arthur Collins interview.] Lenox, Massachusetts. January and June to August, 2005.

Giuffre, Juanita. [Juanita Giuffre interview.] Phone interview, August 7, 2005.

Heath, June. [June Heath interview.] Phone interview, July 31, 2005.

Rollins, Sonny. [Sonny Rollins interview.] Phone interview, August 6, 2005.

Schuller, Gunther. [Gunther Schuller interview.] Phone interview, August 10, 2005.

Weston, Randy. [Randy Weston interview.] Phone interview, September 16, 2006.

NOTES

Introduction

[1] *The Berkshire Herald*, March 14, 1973.

Chapter One

[1] Sonny Rollins interview, August 6, 2005.

Chapter Two

[1] This is Bellefontaine, built in 1899, whose lavish gardens and statuary were destroyed in the 1940s. See *A Pride of Palaces: Lenox Summer Cottages 1883-1933: Sixty Photographs by Edwin Hale Lincoln 1848-1938*, ed. Donald T. Oakes (Lenox, Massachusetts: The Lenox Library Association, 1981), 41.

[2] Clark W. Bryan, *The Book of Berkshire, Describing and Illustrating its Hills and Homes, and Telling Where They Are, What They Are and Why They Are Destined to Become the Most Charming and Desirable Summer Homes in America. For the Season of 1887.* (1886; reprint: North Egremont, Massachusetts: Past Perfect, 1993.

[3] Ibid. Introduction, [p. 5.]

[4] Ibid., [p. 13.]

[5] Mabel Dodge Luhan, *Intimate Memories* (New York: Harcourt, Brace, [1933].

[6] Jean-Louis (Jack Kerouac), "Jazz of the Beat Generation" in *New World Writing* 7 (New York: New American Library, 1955), 7-16. The adoption of a French pseudonym is telling, as some of the first serious critics of jazz – such as Hugues Panassié, Charles Delaunay, and André Hodeir, were French.

[7] Verbal improvisation is captured in Donald Allen, ed., *Composed on the Tongue* (Bolinas, California: Grey Fox, 1980), where Ginsberg explains that his inspiration for *Howl* was also Lester Young, "[a]nd I got that from Kerouac."

[8] This phenomenon continues today, with white suburban youth mimicking the accents and argot of the hip-hop culture.

[9] Norman Mailer, "The White Negro: Superficial Reflections on the Hipster," *Dissent* 4/3 (Summer 1957), 276-93.

[10] Frank O'Hara, "Answer to Voznesensky & Evtushenko" in Frank O'Hara, *Collected Poems* (New York: Knopf, 1972), 468.

[11] Jack Kerouac, *On the Road* (New York: Viking, 1957), 180.

[12] David Meltzer, ed., *Reading Jazz* (San Francisco: Mercury, 1993), 52. Meltzer writes that the desire to take on the attributes of the other race works both ways. "Whites want to become black; blacks want to live unnoticed in the palace of white culture." Ibid., 37.

Chapter Three

[1] *New York Times*, February 5, 1891.

[2] Philip Willson Barber, *The Scene Technician's Handbook* (New York: Whitlock, 1928).

[3] After they were married, in 1947, the Barbers began their adventure in the Berkshires by living in a tent whenever they came up on weekends. Stephanie was not thrilled with this arrangement. They had to shovel the cow dung out of the way to reach their tent. "I hated camping more than anything I've ever done in my life!" The following year they moved into the Old Shaker Mill not far away. Unfortunately it was also home to a large number of mice, about which Stephanie had something of a phobia, inherited from her mother. "I call them 'm's'. I'd rather not say the word." It was only after a year of living with the mice that they sold the Mill and bought the buildings and the land in Lenox. (Barber/Collins interview.)

[4] Benjamin Barber interview. I am grateful to Benjamin Barber for his help and insight into his father's and stepmother's work in founding the Lenox School of Jazz.

[5] Juanita Giuffre interview.

[6] Stephanie Barber interview.

[7] Undated brochure of the Music Inn. Many of the archival materials from the Music Inn are housed at the Lenox Library Association in Lenox, Massachusetts, a generous gift of Willson, Benjamin, Chip, and Hillary Barber and Arthur Collins. Unless otherwise indicated, all references are to this source. Other materials were consulted at the library of the *Berkshire Eagle* in Pittsfield, Massachusetts, and at the Pittsfield Athenaeum. I am extremely grateful to Arthur Collins, Stephanie Barber's second husband, for his graciousness and generosity in providing the documents that are the basis of this

study and for his unfailing willingness to respond to my constant questions.
[8] The designer was Warner Leeds, head of the New York design firm Warner Leeds and Associates.
[9] Berkshire Music Barn program booklet, 1958.
[10] Barber/Collins interview. One thing that Stephanie did like about living in the country was not worrying about what clothes to wear, as she did in the city. "Phil bought me a pair of overalls. It was my outfit, and I never had to think what I had to wear."
[11] Stephanie Barber interview.

Chapter Four

[1] Milton R. Bass, "The Lively Arts," *The Berkshire Evening Eagle*, July 5, 1951. Apparently Bass knew nothing about jazz but became an enthusiast. Marshall Stearns thought that his conversion was "close to a miracle." Unpublished "Chronology of Marshall Winslow Stearns" by James T. Maher. Maher wrote an "appreciation" of Marshall Stearns for the Da Capo reprint of Marshall and Jean Stearns, *Jazz Dance: The Story of American Vernacular Dance* (New York: Da Capo, 1994). Maher is the author of several books and articles about jazz, popular music, and the musical theater.
[2] Barber/Collins interview.
[3] "Chatterbox Says." Undated and unidentifiable clipping filed under 1952 in Music Inn archives.
[4] *Down Beat*, September 7, 1951.
[5] Stephanie Barber interview.
[6] Jules Schwerin, *Got to Tell It: Mahalia Jackson, Queen of Gospel* (New York: Oxford University Press, 1992), 77-8.
[7] Ibid., 79.
[8] Stephanie Barber interview.
[9] Joan Mills, "Mahalia and Stephanie," *Berkshire Eagle*, August 1, 1969.
[10] Philip Barber, "The Concerts at Music Inn: Before the Great Controversy." Unpublished typescript.
[11] *New Orleans Jazz Club* 3, November-December, 1952.
[12] *Record Changer*, August, 1952. The 1953 July-August special issue of the *Record Changer* was devoted entirely to the Institute.
[13] Benjamin Barber interview. Other people also found Jimmy Giuffre to be

an inspiring influence. Perry Robinson, who studied with Giuffre at Lenox in 1959, has written that Giuffre had "a very unique mind always. . . . Just being around Jimmy was wonderful because the feeling of his being was very high; he was very calm, with a burning intensity inside. He was one of the first people I knew who studied Zen, and he had a very Zen quality. He didn't speak a lot; he used no extra verbiage, just like how he played. [Robinson had earlier said: " he didn't play a lot of notes; his style was simple and not at all flashy."] He's a very special man. . . ." Perry Robinson and Florence Wetzel, "The School of Jazz in Lenox, Massachusetts," *Coda* (July/August 2002), 8.

[14] Beth Greiner, "Jazz Circle Found in Square Territory," ?*Boston Globe*, n.d.

[15] Benjamin Barber interview. Barber may have been thinking of later times, because in the beginning Music Inn was careful not to program its musical events at the same time as Tanglewood concerts.

[16] Robert M. Hodesh, "The Musical Berkshires: 'Biggest Summer Culture Foundry in the Country'," *Lincoln-Mercury Times*, May-June, 1955.

[17] *Detroit Chronicle*, August 29, 1959.

[18] *Down Beat*, September 7, 1951.

[19] Robert Bagar, "Berkshire Festival City All Jazzed Up," *New York World-Telegram and Sun*, August 23, 1951.

[20] Unidentifiable newspaper clipping from the Music Inn archives, dated in pencil "1951."

[21] Ibid.

[22] Marshall Stearns, "Roundtable on Jazz," *New York Times*, August 24, 1952.

[23] Quoted in the *Schenectady Gazette*, August 1, 1960.

[24] Benjamin Barber interview.

[25] *Detroit Chronicle*, August 29, 1959.

[26] Seth Rogovoy, "The Life and Times of Music Inn," *Berkshire Magazine*, Summer, 1995, 34.

[27] Barber/Collins interview.

[28] Benjamin Barber interview.

[29] Nat Hentoff, "Not So Random, Not So Festive Thoughts," *Jazz Today*, October, 1957.

[30] http://www.projectilearts.org/musicinn/history/founders.html, accessed June 16, 2005. Forty years later Seeger still remembered this moment. In a

letter to Stephanie Barber for a 1998 celebration of Music Inn, he described the era as "the Frightened Fifties."

Chapter Five

[1] *Secretariat News*, November 16, 1953.

[2] "Blues in the Night" (unsigned article), *The Springfield* [Massachusetts] *Sunday Republican*, September 20, 1953.]

[3] Benjamin Barber interview.

[4] Private communication.

[5] "The Berkshires: Sports, Scenery, and Culture, too," *Cue*, Spring, 1953.

[6] Milton R. Bass, "The Lively Arts," *The Berkshire Evening Eagle*, September 19, 1953.

[7] "Music Inn: They Come to Play" (unsigned article), *Business Week*, September 19, 1953.

[8] Ibid.

[9] Ibid.

[10] Ibid.

[11] *Cue*, Spring, 1953.

[12] Brian F. King, "Bop on Wane, Blues Back Says Exposition Headliner," *Springfield* [Massachusetts] *Sunday Republican*, September 27, 1953.

[13] Richard Gehman, "The Jazz Scholar," *The New York Herald Tribune*, May 9, 1954.

[14] Roger Maren, "A Few False Notes at Newport," *The Reporter*, September 8, 1955.

Chapter Six

[1] Seth Rogovoy, "The Life and Times," 36. Stephanie also recalled that she was "ashamed" at having all these musicians at the Inn and not being able to pay them properly. "Music Barn was a way of paying them."

[2] Barber/Collins interview.

[3] Dyer-Bennet was to appear every summer at the Music Barn until 1959. Known as the "twentieth-century troubadour," he was a nationally known singer, who had a repertoire of over 800 folk- and art-songs from various nations around the world. He sang every year in Carnegie Hall to capacity audiences. See *The Berkshire Eagle*, July 16, 1959.

[4] *I Like Jazz!* (Columbia JZ 1) was a compilation, featuring Wally Rose, Bessie Smith, Louis Armstrong, Bix Beiderbecke, Eddie Condon, Frankie Trumbauer, Pete Rugolo, Benny Goodman, Phil Napoleon, Turk Murphy, Duke Ellington, Teddy Wilson, Billie Holiday, and Dave Brubeck. By the mid Fifties, Columbia, having noted how profitable jazz was becoming, was eager to expand its jazz catalogue and did so by signing promising players such as Miles Davis, who left Prestige to join Columbia in 1955.

[5] Cowell's comments were reproduced in part from an issue of *The Record Changer* (July-August, 1953), which was devoted to the Institute of Jazz Studies. A section of the issue with comments by several authors is simply entitled "Additional Commentary." Cowell's piece appears on p. 19. It is not listed in the Cowell bibliography: Bruce Saylor, *The Writings of Henry Cowell: A Descriptive Bibliography*, Institute for Studies in American Music Monographs, no. 7 (Brooklyn, New York: Institute for Studies in American Music, 1977). In 1955 Reisner also served as the first manager of the Music Barn. Stephanie remembered that when he first arrived at the Inn, he was put up in the attic of the Barn with his new wife. The next morning the housekeeper found the two of them in the linen closet making love. They slept there for the rest of their stay, because they couldn't deal with bats on their honeymoon. Stephanie Barber interview.

[6] Howard Taubman, "Country Jazz," *New York Times*, August 7, 1955.

[7] Nat Hentoff, "Counterpoint," *Down Beat* (June 1, 1955), 25.

[8] Paul D. Coss, "Barn Dance in Lenox That's Something Else," *Metronome* (September, 1955), 8.

[9] Dorothy Roe, "Blonde Converts Barn to Profit," Asbury Park, New Jersey, *Press*, July 22, 1955; also appearing under the headline "It's Possible to Convert the Culture-Conscious to Jazz" in the Morristown, New Jersey, *Record*; as "Jazz in the Berkshires Offers Lively Contrast" in the New Brunswick, New Jersey, *Home News*, on the same date; as "New Yorker Adds Jazz to Fare at Berkshires" in the Charlotte, North Carolina, *Observer* as "City Girl Brings Jazz to Folks in Berkshires" in the New Haven, Connecticut, *Register* on July 24, 1955; and as "She Sends Long-Hairs to Cover" in the St. Paul, Minnesota, *Dispatch*, on July 26, 1955.

[10] "Smart of Mind and Smart of Dress," Pittsfield, Massachusetts, *Berkshire Eagle*, September 13, 1956.

[11] Benjamin Barber says that his father "approached the place with a certain dramatic flair – hence the wall of speakers. He was also in public relations and was good at marketing the new institutions." (Benjamin Barber interview.)

Chapter Seven

[1] *The Berkshire Eagle*, July 2, 1956.

[2] Stephanie Barber interview.

[3] *The Tanglewood Times*, Summer, 1956.

[4] Ibid.

[5] Barber/Collins interview.

[6] June Heath interview. Mrs. Heath also reminisced about the first time the MJQ played in London. The stage manager of the hall had provided John Lewis with a piano that had seen better days. Over in the corner was a shiny new Steinway concert grand. When Lewis asked if he could use the Steinway instead, the stage manager said, in a very haughty English accent, "Oh no, that's for *proper* music." The story ends happily, however. At the end of the concert, the stage manager said that Lewis was welcome to use the Steinway the next time the group played there.

[7] Barber/Collins interview.

[8] Marshall W. Stearns, *The Story of Jazz* (New York: Oxford University Press, 1956).

[9] Robert Reisner, "Reminiscences of Marshall Stearns," *Journal of Jazz Studies* 1 (1973), 84-9.

[10] The appearance of the Max Roach Quintet on July 12 followed by two weeks the car accident that killed the brilliant young talents (and Roach combo members) pianist Richie Powell and trumpeter Clifford Brown at the ages of 25 and 26 respectively. They had appeared at Lenox the year before. The Music Barn concert was dedicated to their memory.

[11] New York: Prentice-Hall, [1954].

[12] "A Musical Map – Summer 1956," *New York Times*, June 3, 1956.

[13] Stephanie Barber interview.

[14] Warner Music Japan MTCJ-6005 (WQCP-214).

[15] Seth Rogovoy, "The Life and Times," 36. The Giuffres bought an old mill on the river in West Stockbridge called The Stone Mill.

[16] More photographs of Giuffre at the Music Inn, playing both clarinet and tenor saxophone, are reproduced for the Mosaic box set *The Complete Capitol and Atlantic Recordings of Jimmy Giuffre* (Mosaic MD6-176).

[17] Juanita Giuffre interview.

[18] The three tracks featuring Giuffre, however, can be heard on the Mosaic box set mentioned above.

[19] Wilder Hobson, "The Amen Corner: Soft Airs," *Saturday Review*, May, 1959.

[20] *The Teddy Charles Tentet*, Atlantic 1229.

[21] Stephanie Barber interview.

[22] Dizzy Gillespie, *To Be, or Not . . . to Bop* (New York: Da Capo, 1985), 404.

[23] *Metronome*, November, 1956; *Down Beat*, October 17, 1956; *Jazz Today*, December, 1956, and July and August, 1957. The last two contain the most extensive transcripts.

[24] Reported in *Down Beat*, October 17, 1956.

[25] According to Stephanie Barber, her husband said that something should come out of the discussions, and both John Lewis and Stephanie "practically said it together: 'The School of Jazz!'" (Barber/Collins interview.)

Chapter Eight

[1] John S. Wilson, liner notes to Atlantic 1247; "Music Inn Owners Will Buy Wheatleigh," *The Berkshire Eagle*, November 13, 1957.

[2] *Hommes et problèmes du jazz* was originally written in 1954 but appeared in English two years later as *Jazz: Its Evolution and Essence* (New York: Grove, 1956).

[3] Stephanie Barber interview.

[4] *Metronome*, April, 1957. Announcement of the upcoming session was made in *Variety*, and *Jazz Today* editorialized: "We have an interior siren, which sounds when we are about to begin a sentence with such a phrase as, 'This is probably the most important step taken in jazz . . .'" And, yet, there is no doubt in our minds that the newly announced *The School of Jazz* is that kind of step." "Beret and Goatee to Play 2d Fiddle to Cap and Gown as Jazz Goes to School," *Variety* (February 6, 1957), 49; *Jazz Today*, May, 1957.

[5] http://www.projectilearts.org/musicinn/history/jazzschool.html, accessed August 7, 2005.

[6] Much of the following information is based on the archive at the Lenox

Library Association as well as on the research of Michael Fitzgerald. See his website "The Lenox School of Jazz," http://www. jazzdiscography.com/Lenox/ lenhome.htm, accessed July 3, 2005.

[7] *Down Beat*, October 3, 1957.

[8] "The School of Jazz: A Practical Approach to Music Education," *Metronome*, October, 1958.

[9] "Jazz Swings at Music Inn Jazz School," *Metronome*, July, 1957.

[10] *Down Beat*, October 3, 1957.

[11] "Jumping Juilliard," *Harper's Magazine*, November, 1957, 82-3; "Jazz without Juleps," *Newsweek*, September 1, 1958; "The School of Jazz, Part II: A Practical Approach to Music Education," *Metronome*, November, 1958.

[12] Ron Riddle, "A Look Back at Lenox," *Jazz: A Quarterly of American Music*, October, 1958.

[13] June Heath interview.

[14] F. Tupper Saussy, *The Miracle on Main Street: Saving Yourself and America from Financial Ruin*, 6th ed. (Sewanee, Tennessee: Spencer Judd, 1984), and idem, *Rulers Of Evil* (New York: HarperCollins, 1999).

[15] For a complete listing of the students, see Michael Fitzgerald's website http://www.jazzdiscography.com/Lenox/students.htm, accessed July 17, 2005.

[16] "Exposure" was Lewis's score to a United Nations documentary film of the same name.

[17] *The Tanglewood Times*, Summer, 1957.

[18] Berkshire Music Barn program book, 1957. Dinner, supper, and drinks menus for the Potting Shed (undated).

[19] Nat Hentoff, "The Tanglewood Jazz School," *Saturday Review* (September 14, 1957), 66.

[20] "The School of Jazz," *Down Beat* (October 3, 1957), 23.

[21] *Harper's Magazine*, November, 1957.

[22] Nat Hentoff, "A Civilian's Report: Jazz Scholarships, Anyone?," *Metronome*, December, 1957.

Chapter Nine

[1] "Music Inn Owners Will Buy Wheatleigh," *The Berkshire Eagle*, November 13, 1957.

[2] Typescript of Jules Foster's speech entitled "Some Words on the Topic

'What is a Liberal Education in Music?'" See also an abridged version of the discussion printed in *Metronome*, October, 1958.

3 "90 Places of Interest: What to See and Do," *Life*, May 26, 1958.

4 "Music Inn Opens Season June 27," *Boston Sunday Herald*, June 8, 1958. Unfortunately the water tower was destroyed by fire in 1990.

5 "Articulate Innkeeper Discusses Her Fashion Philosophy," *Berkshire Eagle*, June 27, 1958.

6 "Jazz Seminar," *Ebony*, November 1957; Lydia T. Brown, "The Yankee Traveller," *Afro-American*, July 26, 1958.

7 Richard V. Happel, "Ice-House Barbers Score with Cool Jazz," *The Berkshire Eagle*, August 9, 1958.

8 The swimming pool was added in 1961.

9 Members of the faculty and musicians in residence were announced in *Down Beat*. "Profs with a Purpose," *Down Beat* (July 10, 1958), 9.

10 Folkways 2801-2811.

11 Riverside SDP 11.

12 Columbia 919.

13 Capitol 793-6.

14 Folkways FC 7312.

15 New York: Durrell, 1947.

16 New York: Citadel, 1948.

17 New York: Arrow, 1938.

18 Leonard Feather, *The Book of Jazz: A Guide to the Entire Field* (New York: Horizon, 1957).

19 "The School of Jazz, Part II: A Practical Approach to Music Education," *Metronome*, November, 1958.

20 Quoted in Bob Brookmeyer "The School of Jazz: Faculty Views," *Jazz Review*, February, 1959.

21 *Max Roach with the Boston Percussion Ensemble under the Direction of Harold Farberman*, Mercury MG 36144.

22 "Music Inn Suite Record Released by Mercury Co.," *The Berkshire Eagle*, March 26, 1959.

23 Recording of this concert was shared by Metrojazz, a subsidiary of MGM that lasted less than a year and only produced fifteen albums. Metrojazz E-1011 has *Teddy Edwards at the Falcon's Lair* on one side and *Sonny Rollins with*

the Modern Jazz Quartet at the Music Inn on the other. (See the Metrojazz discography compiled by Mike Callahan and David Edwards at http://www. iconnect.net/home/bsnpubs/mgm/ metrojazz.html.)

[24] Gunther Schuller went on to become the head of the faculty at Tanglewood in 1963, where he stayed for over twenty years, and president of the New England Conservatory from 1967 to 1977.

[25] See *New Grove Dictionary of Jazz*, 2nd ed. (London: Macmillan, 2002), "Herman, Woody" s.v.

[26] All of the tracks from this album are also available on the Mosaic box set. The recording in Lenox was made with Giuffre playing one saxophone. The overdubs were recorded in the Atlantic studios in New York. Atlantic's engineer at that time was Tom Dowd, who was a pioneer in stereo and overdubbing techniques. The student concert from 1958 was even recorded in stereo.

[27] "Jazz without Juleps," *Newsweek*, September 1, 1958.

[28] *School of Jazz*, October, 1958. Lewis added that they did so "because they believe in the School."

[29] "The School of Jazz: A Practical Approach to Music Education," *Metronome*, October, 1958; "The School of Jazz, Part II: A Practical Approach to Music Education," *Metronome*, November, 1958.

[30] "The Lenox School of Jazz," *Down Beat* (November 13, 1958), 20.

Chapter Ten

[1] *Esquire*, January, 1959; the duet may be heard on *Historic Jazz Concert at Music Inn* (Atlantic 1298) and on the Giuffre Mosaic set mentioned above (see footnote 16 on p.145).

[2] John Clellon Holmes, *Go* (Mamaroneck, New York: Appel, 1952).

[3] "This Is the Beat Generation: A 26-year-old Defines his Times" *New York Times* Magazine, November 16,1952; http://www.rooknet.com/beatpage/writers/ holmes.html, accessed September 27, 2004.

[4] *The Annual Register of Distinctive Dining in City and Country 1959*, published by *Cue* magazine.

[5] "Soft Airs," *Saturday Review*, May, 1959.

[6] Patrick Chase, "Playboy's International Datebook," *Playboy*, May, 1959.

7 *The Berkshire Eagle*, February 24, 1959. Apparently the owner of the company, Rudy Schaefer, was a jazz buff. The scholarships were announced in *Down Beat*. "Lenox Gets a Head," *Down Beat* (March 19, 1959), 9.

8 "John Lewis Chair Established," *Chattanooga* [Tennessee] *Observer*, July 3, 1959.

9 *The Berkshire Eagle*, August 22, 1959.

10 Ralph J. Gleason, "The School of Jazz Deserves Some Help," *San Francisco Chronicle*, c. March 25, 1959.

11 George Frazier, "The Story of Jazz," *Coronet*, March, 1959.

12 *The Berkshire Eagle*, June 9, 1959.

13 "Illness Cancels Lenox Concert," *Springfield* [Massachusetts] *Union*, June 24, 1959.

14 *The Berkshire Eagle*, June 25, 1959.

15 http://nfo.net/usa/b7.html, accessed June 22, 2005.

16 *The Lakeville Journal*, July 2, 1959.

17 *The Berkshire Eagle*, July 8, 1959.

18 *Lakeville* [Connecticut] *Journal*, July 9, 1959.

19 Holyoke, [Massachusetts] *Transcript Telegram*, July 14, 1959.

20 *The Berkshire Eagle*, July 13, 1959.

21 *The Berkshire Eagle*, July 20, 1959.

22 *The Berkshire Eagle*, July 23, 1959.

23 *Holyoke* [Massachusetts] *Transcript Telegram*, July 29, 1959.

24 Ibid.

25 *The Berkshire Eagle*, July 31, 1959. "Letters," *The Berkshire Eagle*, August 3 and August 6, 1959.

26 "Jazz Notes," *Lakeville* [Connecticut] *Journal*, August 13, 1959.

27 Stephanie Barber interview. It should be noted that nobody has confirmed the story of Davis playing for the students and staff in the fields in the middle of the night.

28 *The Berkshire Eagle*, August 24, 1959.

29 *Lakeville* [Connecticut] *Journal*, August 27, 1959.

30 *The Berkshire Eagle*, August 3, 1959.

31 *The Berkshire Eagle*, August 12, 1959.

32 *The Berkshire Eagle*, August 31, 1959.

33 Sonny Rollins interview.

[34] *The Berkshire Eagle*, September 8, 1959.

[35] *Springfield* [Massachusetts] *Republican*, July 19, 1959.

[36] *Minneapolis Tribune*, July 19, 1959.

[37] Nat Hentoff, "Cool School for Hot Jazz," *Today's Living: The Herald Tribune Magazine*, July 26, 1959.

[38] "Unique Jazz School Opens in Lenox," *Boston Herald*, August 16, 1959.

[39] "Jazz School Is Harder Than College," *Washington Post and Times Herald*, August 24, 1959.

[40] "School of Jazz Students Find Learning Is Work," *Hartford Courant*, August 23, 1959.

[41] *The Berkshire Eagle*, August 22, 1959.

[42] *The Berkshire Eagle*, August 27, 1959. Stephanie remembered that one day "in alarm" she saw Jimmy and Juanita sitting on the couch holding hands. (Stephanie Barber interview.) However the Russells and the Giuffres remained fast friends after the re-shuffle. Juanita Giuffre says that they had "so much respect for each other's music." (Juanita Giuffre interview.)]

[43] Perry Robinson has also written a book about his life, which contains a substantial passage on the School of Jazz: Perry Robinson and Florence Wetzel, *Perry Robinson: The Traveler* (Lincoln, Nebraska: Writers Club, 2002). The passage is excerpted as "The School of Jazz in Lenox, Massachusetts" in *Coda* (July/August 2002): 7-9.

[44] Once again, I am indebted to Michael Fitzgerald's website http://www.jazzdiscography.com/Lenox/lenhome.htm, accessed June 28, 2005.

[45] *New York Herald Tribune*, August 30, 1959.

[46] Alyn Shipton, *A New History of Jazz* (London: Continuum, 2001), 774.

[47] A. B. Spellman, *Four Lives in the Bebop Business* ([London]: MacGibbon and Kee, 1967), 81.

[48] *Springfield* [Massachusetts] *Sunday Republican*, September 6, 1959. The caption referred to Cherry as a "boy." Let us assume that this was because of his youth rather than because of his race, although Miles Davis (to his fury) was described as "the boy who played so beautifully" by the organizer of the Newport Jazz Festival. See Scott DeVeaux, review of *Miles: The Autobiography* in *American Music* 10 (1992), 93.

[49] Gunther Schuller, (first of) "Two Reports on the School of Jazz," *Jazz Review*, November 1960.

[50] See Lorin Stephens, "An Interview with Jimmy Giuffre: The Passionate

Conviction," *Jazz Review*, February, 1960. Perry Robinson, who was a clarinet student of Giuffre's in 1959, has written that when Giuffre heard Coleman that summer, "it blew his mind. One time there was a jam session going on with George Russell and Ornette, and I was watching through the window. Jimmy was standing there listening, and after Ornette took his solo Jimmy fell on the floor and started kicking his feet. He had such an amazing reaction to the music, it was like an orgasm." Perry Robinson and Florence Wetzel, "The School of Jazz in Lenox, Massachusetts," *Coda* (July/August 2002), 8.

[51] John Litweiler, *The Freedom Principle: Jazz after 1958* (New York: William Morrow, 1984), 54.

[52] *The Berkshire Eagle*, September 10, 1959.

[53] Gunther Schuller, (first of) "Two Reports," 14.

[54] Ornette Coleman interview.

[55] *The Berkshire Eagle*, August 31, 1959.

[56] "Report on Lenox," *Down Beat* (October 15, 1959), 11.

[57] Martin Williams, "A Letter from Lenox, Mass.," *Jazz Review*, October 1959.

[58] The play list in full is as follows: David Baker's "Lone Ranger and the Great Horace Silver," Gary McFarland's "Monk's Sphere," Al Kiger's arrangement of Wes Montgomery's "Jingles," Kenny Dorham's "D. C. Special," Coleman's "The Sphinx," Margo Guryan's "Inn Tune," George Russell's "Stratusphunk," Jimmy Giuffre's "Ray's Time," Bobby Freedman's "To Thee, O Asphodel," Sonny Rollins's "Paul's Pal," and Danny Kent's "Blue Grass." The program for the entire concert may be seen in Appendix 5.

[59] Just these two tunes from the private recording are available on Royal Jazz SOJ 1/2, RJD 513[CD].

[60] Jack Maher, "The School of Jazz: Amazing Talent Marks Third Year," *Metronome*, October, 1959, 14.

[61] "Report on Lenox," *Down Beat* (October 15, 1959), 11.

[62] Thomas Pynchon, *V* (Philadelphia: Lippincott, 1963), 59-60, 292, 298.

[63] "Modern Living: Festivals of Music, Drama and Art Offer Varied Summer Entertainment," *Danbury* [Connecticut] *News-Times*, June 25, 1959. Wein even hired Marshall Stearns to lecture at Newport.

[64] Ralph J. Gleason, "Jazz Festivals On Increase," *Philadelphia Bulletin*, July 5, 1959.

[65] Stephanie remembered that Josh White "taught me the naughtiest song

that I ever heard. I heard him singing it, and I said, 'You can't sing that in public,' and he said, 'I'll teach it to you then.' 'One foot on the ceiling, one foot on the floor. [If that don't get a baby, don't come back no more.] I'm going to rub your tummy, Baby, until your eyes turn cherry red. [When your baby comes a'callin' you're gonna fall right out of bed.]" (Stephanie Barber interview.)

[66] *Down Beat*, July 9, 1959.

[67] Stephanie Barber interview. The concert was by the Stan Kenton Orchestra.

[68] Bill Matney, "Views of the News," *Detroit Chronicle*, August 29, 1959.

[69] http://www.berkshireweb.com/rogovoy/interviews/barbers.html, accessed July 1, 2005.

[70] Stephanie Barber interview.

[71] Remarks at the dinner honoring Stephanie Barber and the School of Jazz at the National Music Foundation, Lenox, Massachusetts, August 20, 1998. Gunther Schuller feels that many young black musicians at that time were gravitating to rhythm and blues rather than to jazz. (Gunther Schuller interview.)

[72] Diane Gordon, "Black History and the Shire," *Berkshire Eagle*, January 24, 2004.

[73] *Brooklyn Record*, August 14, 1959.

[74] Milton Bass, "Substitute Program at Music Barn," *The Berkshire Eagle*, August 10, 1959.

[75] Barry Ulanov, "Women in Jazz: Do They Belong?" *Down Beat* (January 9, 1958), 17.

[76] Russ Wilson, "Mystery Surrounds Film Cancellation," *Oakland Tribune*, August 30, 1959.

[77] Sony 57663.

[78] However the following year Berendt collaborated with photographer William Claxton on a cross-country photo journal with the same premise as the movie. This resulted in a book that was published as *Jazz Life* (Offenburg: Burda, 1961).

[79] "Then in 1950 the man who had always arranged for my appearances in the colored churches in New York told me about a symposium on the origins of jazz music that was going to be held up in Massachusetts. Music

professors from the Juilliard School of Music, Columbia University and a lot
of other big places had been invited; and they wanted me to some up and
sing some gospel songs for them. . . . As soon as I finished [singing], a great
big fuss busted loose. The professors started arguing with one another and
asking me [all kinds of questions]. They kept me there half the night. . . .
What happened was that we stayed on for a whole week while the professors
asked me questions about colored church music; blues singers; field calls and
chants. . . . I went back to Chicago, and everything started happening at once.
. . . Requests came pouring in. . . . Ed Sullivan . . . Carnegie Hall . . ." Mahalia
Jackson (as told to Evan McLeod Wylie), "I Can't Stop Singing," *The Saturday
Evening Post*, December 5, 1959.

80 *Life*, December 28, 1959.

81 Ibid.

82 *The Berkshire Eagle*, February 19, 1960.

Chapter Eleven

1 *Berkshire Eagle*, August 1, 8, 15, 22, and 29, 1960.

2 *The Berkshire Eagle*, August 24, 1960; an article in *Down Beat* referred to
Bakwin as "a jazz angel." "The School at Lenox," *Down Beat* (November 10,
1960), 12.

3 Schuller first used the term in a lecture at Brandeis University. See the
New Grove Dictionary of Jazz, "Third Stream" s.v.

4 In one of the panel discussions at the Music Inn in 1956 the talk turned
to the relationship between jazz and classical music. "A tentative agreement
was reached that there would be a fusion of classical technique with jazz, as
there already has been, but that no attempt to meld the two musical strains
was advisable." "The Composer in Jazz: More Time for Deep Thought," *Jazz
Today*, December, 1956.

5 *The Berkshire Eagle*, September 2, 1960.

6 Gunther Schuller and Don Heckman, "Two Reports on the School of Jazz,"
Jazz Review, November, 1960, 14-19.

7 June Heath told me that she had been "nine and a half months pregnant"
when they were in Lenox that summer. (June Heath interview.)

Chapter Twelve

[1] *The Berkshire Eagle*, September 2, 1960; "The School at Lenox," *Down Beat* (November 10, 1960), 13.

[2] Stephanie Barber interview.

[3] Schuller interview.

[4] 36 in 1957, 34 in 1958, 43 in 1959, 45 in 1960. http://www.jazzdiscography. com/ Lenox/lenhome.html, accessed August 17, 2005.

[5] http://www.berkshireweb.com/rogovoy/interviews/barber2.html,accessed July1,2005. Weston calls the Music Inn "my second spiritual home." See http:// www. projectilearts.org/musicinn/history/index.html, accessed July 1, 2005.

[6] Letter from Lisa Thaler to Stephanie Barber, dated May 24, 2000.

[7] The portrait is reproduced on the cover of *Touché: The Literary-Humor Magazine of Bucknell University* [n.d. 1960?], and some other sketches as well as a relaxed painting of Dizzy Gillespie and Max Roach playing chess on the grass are reproduced inside the magazine (pp. 8-9).

[8] Seth Rogovoy, "The Life and Times," 34.

[9] Ibid.

[10] Information about Martha Schlamme is uncertain, as no reviews can be found.

[11] Sony 8210. Olatunji's autobiography was published in 2005. In it he mentions his time at the "Tanglewood Music Festival." See Babatunde Olatunji, *The Beat of My Drum: An Autobiography* (Philadelphia: Temple University Press, 2005), 117-18.

[12] "It was a miniature Woodstock for 10 years," said Lenox photographer Michael Flower, who regularly attended the concerts in the '70s. "It was really quite bizarre." See Stephen Leon, "The Day the Music Died," *Berkshires Week*, August 23-29, 1985.

[13] Ibid.

[14] Ibid.

[15] Ibid.

[16] Stephanie Barber interview.

[17] Anne Edwards and Stephen Citron, *The Inn and Us* (New York: Random House, 1976), 28, 31, 33.

Chapter Thirteen

[1] *Berkshire Courier*, August 21, 1975. 1975 was, however, the twentieth anniversary of the first appearance of the Modern Jazz Quartet at the Music Barn in 1955.

[2] *Berkshire Eagle*, August 18, 1975.

[3] Juanita Giuffre also composed music. One of her tunes, "J to J," is on Giuffre's *Dragonfly* album (Soul Note 121058.)

[4] Seth Rogovoy, "For Jazzmen Lewis and Marsalis, It's a Lifelong Affair with Lenox," *Berkshires Week*, October 10, 1996, 12.

[5] Ibid.

[6] Ben Ratliff, "Recalling the Gentle Elegance of John Lewis, Jazzman," *New York Times*, April 9, 2001.

[7] Letter from Lisa Thaler to Stephanie Barber, dated May 24, 2000.

[8] Seth Rogovoy, "The Life and Times."

[9] Letter of October 5, 1995.

[10] http://www.berkshireweb.com/rogovoy/other/musicinn_note.html, accessed July 13, 2005.

[11] Gennari's book *Blowin' Hot and Cool: Jazz and Its Critics* (Chicago: Chicago University Press, 2006) appeared just as this volume was going to press. The School is discussed on pp. 219-25 of that book.

[12] Richard Houdek, "Music Inn," *Berkshire Home Style* (January 2006), 14.

[13] "The Lenox School of Jazz," http://www.jazzdiscography. com/Lenox/lenhome.htm, accessed July 21, 2005. Some of this material was published as "The Lenox School of Jazz," *Jazz Education Journal* 35 (2002): 48-51, and the International Association for Jazz Education posted it on its website http://www.iaje.org/article.asp? ArticleID=111, dated September 2002, accessed August 22, 2005.

[14] Hentoff wrote that "a phenomenon unto itself was the time I spent at Music Inn. I learned so much during those days and nights that I have been mining that information ever since." The Giuffres recalled it as "a time of revelation, discourse, and just plain happiness."

[15] A brief summary of the discussion is given at http://www.jazzhouse.org/library/index. php3?read=robinson2, accessed August 22, 2005.

[16] http://www.projectilearts.org/musicinn/film/producers.html, accessed July 29, 2005. The project and a capsule history of the Music Inn are mentioned

in Elliott Simon, "Modern Jazz Quartet: The Music Inn," *All About Jazz: New York*, November 5, 2003, also posted at http://www.allaboutjazz.com/php/ article.php?id=454, accessed August 22, 2005. A promotional trailer for the film may be seen at http://www.projectilearts.org/musicinn/music_inn_ promo.html.

[17] Ibid.

[18] http://www.berkshireweb.com/rogovoy/interviews/barber.html, accessed August 5, 2005.

[19] Sonny Rollins interview.

[20] Private communication.

[21] Darius Brubeck, "David Baker and the Lenox School of Jazz," *Jazz Education Journal*, September 2002.

[22] Randy Weston interview.

[23] Gunther Schuller interview.

ILLUSTRATION CREDITS

p. 15   Berkshire Music Barn program, 1963

pp. 17, 18, 22, 126   Susanna Yudkin

p. 24   William E. Mahan

p. 25   Ed Bride

p. 29   Richard Saunders

p. 33   *Ebony* Magazine, November 1957

pp. 37, 40, 43 (top), 65, 77, 80, 94   Lenox Library Association, Music Inn
    archive

p. 43   (bottom)   *The Berkshire Eagle*, Sept. 13, 1955

p. 45   Warren Fowler

p. 46   Berkshire Music Barn program, 1962.

p. 51   Mosaic MD6-176

p. 63   Atlantic 1345

p. 74   Atlantic 1299

p. 88   *Jazz Review*, October 1959

p. 97   Springfield (Mass.) *Sunday Republican*, Sept. 6, 1959

p. 102   *The Saturday Evening Post*, Dec. 5, 1959

p. 107   *Business Week*, Sept. 19, 1953

p. 112   Courtesy June Heath

p. 119   Courtesy Juanita Guiffre

p. 122   Berkshire Music Barn program, 1960

A NOTE ON THE TYPE

This book is set in Fairfield Medium. Rudolf Ruzicka's font, from 1939, was based closely on historical antecedents but expressed the spirit of the first half of the Twentieth Century. It was a departure from ornament and imitation of style and a move towards clear simplicity without flourish or embellishment.

Formal details, borrowing heavily from the designs of Art Deco, give Fairfield font its characteristic appearance. The balanced proportions of uppercase and lowercase letters, x-heights, ascenders and descenders result in a font that is both elegant and easy to read.

Jeremy Yudkin is a professor in the Department of Musicology and associated faculty in the Department of African American Studies at Boston University. He is also Visiting Professor of Music at Oxford University. He has been a recipient of Fellowships from the National Endowment for the Humanities, the Whiting Foundation, and the Camargo Foundation. His fields of expertise include the music of Beethoven, medieval music, and jazz. He is the author, among other books, of *Music in Medieval Europe* (Prentice Hall, 1989), *Understanding Music* (Pearson, 1996), and *Miles Davis, "Miles Smiles," and the Invention of Post Bop* (Indiana University Press, 2007). He serves on the advisory panel for the new Smithsonian Collection of Classic Jazz and is a consultant on jazz to the Oxford English Dictionary. He is the founder and teacher of the Summer Music Seminars in Lenox, Massachusetts. He and his family make their home in the Berkshires.